The Bible, Wisdom and Human Nature

Developing the Waverley Model of Counselling

Dr Owen Ashley

WAVERLEY ABBEY
COLLEGE

Copyright © CWR 2015

This printed edition published 2017 by CWR, Waverley Abbey House, Waverley Lane, Farnham, Surrey GU9 8EP, UK. CWR is a Registered Charity – Number 294387 and a Limited Company registered in England – Registration Number 1990308.

Reprinted 2017, 2019, 2020.

The right of Dr Owen Ashley to be identified as the author of this work has been asserted by him in accordance with the Copyright, Designs and Patents Act 1988, sections 77 and 78.

For list of National Distributors visit waverleyabbeyresources.org/national-distributors

Unless otherwise indicated, all Scripture references are from the Holy Bible, New International Version® Anglicised, NIV® Copyright © 1979, 1984, 2011 by Biblica, Inc.® Used by permission. All rights reserved worldwide.

Concept development, editing, design and production by CWR.

Cover Image: pexels.com

Printed in England by 4edge.

ISBN: 978-1-78259-761-2

Contents

Foreword

A brief introduction to the Waverley Model of Counselling

The Waverley Model of Counselling was formulated by Selwyn Hughes (1928–2006) in the early 1980s. Previously, in the 1950s, after undergoing training, Hughes became a pastor within the Assemblies of God branch of Pentecostalism. His father had been converted amidst the Welsh Revival and traces of this background can be seen in his model, which centres on a revival of the personality through greater dependence on God. Initially, Hughes' approach to counselling appeared to be similar to that of Jay Adams, placing all problems under the headings of sin or sickness. However, as a result of his own 'breakdown' and subsequent attendance at Rosemead Graduate School in the USA, a deep appreciation of a third category of 'weakness' or 'infirmity' was added. Hurding describes the Waverley Model as a Christian integrative model, founded upon a biblical world-view, yet open to insights from the psychological sciences.

Hughes regards the deepest needs of people as their longings for security, self-worth and significance, and he maintains that these needs become primary motivators causing problems throughout the personality when they are not met in a relationship with God. Believing that these longings will never be fully satisfied outside of a relationship with God through Christ, the goal of the model therefore becomes helping people move from self-centredness to Christ-centredness.

For Hughes, the counselling process is divided into three phases. Phase one involves an exploration of the presenting problem, plus a general exploration of the client's past history and present circumstances via the 'Ten Basic Life Areas'. Having gained a good overview of the client, phase two proceeds by a systematic attempt to analyse what is happening in each of the 'five areas of functioning' – starting with the 'outer layer' (physical) and ending with the spiritual 'core'. The aim of this is to end phase two by arriving at an understanding of relevant issues from a biblical perspective (diagnosis).

Phase three attempts to work out solutions by reversing the direction undertaken in phase two analysis. Starting with the spiritual area and working through each successive area, new insights and practices are encouraged.

Hughes' legacy

Alongside counselling training, Hughes built CWR into a successful publishing ministry, of which the daily devotional Bible reading notes Every Day with Jesus is the best known, most widely read CWR publication, (one million copies in over 150 countries) and has been in operation for over forty years.

Hughes remained strong in his faith despite the death of his wife in 1986 from cancer, and the deaths of his two sons. His autobiography, My Story, was published in 2004 and a year later Brunel University awarded him an honorary Doctorate of Divinity for his contribution towards Christian education. Selwyn Hughes died of cancer in January 2006.

In recent years, subsequent to his death, Hughes' legacy has continued to develop and expand. In 2010, CWR inaugurated its first degree programme in counselling, validated by Roehampton University. This course gained such popularity that CWR purchased additional premises (Pilgrim Hall in East Sussex) in order to cope with the extra student numbers. In 2014, Waverley Abbey College was opened, which provides Higher Education programmes alongside short courses – all underpinned by a Christian world-view.

My hope is that this book, in addition to fulfilling the following purposes, will also represent a positive contribution to Hughes' legacy.

Purposes of this book

The motivation to write a PhD – the origin of this book – emerged out of my working contexts at CWR and London School of Theology. In particular, the ongoing departmental debate regarding strengths and weaknesses of the Waverley Model of Counselling was a critical context out of which grew my own questions and dissatisfaction with the level of understanding with which I worked at this time.

This book argues for one key modification to the traditional Waverley model of personhood, which promotes a modernist isolated self. The proposal is made that the model needs to better portray the self as essentially dialogical with regard to our continual connectedness to the world 'outside' the self. Such an interrelated self better portrays the historical and ongoing influence upon the self with regard to that which we encounter. With this central emphasis, it should not be surprising to note that the experience of writing this book has had a profound personal impact. One example of internal context is that of my impaired vision, which has made writing difficult and sifting the vast amounts of information extremely arduous. The strain of this has impacted stress levels and concomitant headaches and other bodily strains. Whilst I have been keenly aware of each moment's 'will to act' to sustain the pursuit of completing this work, I have also been profoundly aware of the essential influence of external factors, without which this work would not have been undertaken.

Dr Owen Ashley

Introduction

We are all on a journey of discovery when it comes to the matters of the soul and it is always good to question what we are saying and doing in relation to helping people with their problems.[1] (Selwyn Hughes)

No final or closed model of counselling will ever be developed by fallen finite man. The best model will always have ragged edges which can be partially smoothed out only through openness to new thinking and data.[2] (Larry Crabb)

human knowledge is inevitably fallible (at least on this side of the eschaton). It is always in process, partial, perspectival, and infected with finitude. It is never infallible, absolute, and exhaustive.[3] (Amos Young)

In light of the above quotations, it may be regarded as always appropriate to reassess the ideas that we hold to be true at any given point in time. After all, to treat something as if it is perfect, beyond correction, runs the risk of idolatry – only God Himself is perfect, our ideas, even if rooted in Scripture are not. In general, I have a very positive regard for Selwyn Hughes' Waverley Model of Counselling, in part because I have personally found it very helpful in making sense of aspects of my own life. Yet I am increasingly aware of both its strengths and weaknesses (raggedness) arising from my own reading and reflections, as well as the many questions posed by both students and teaching colleagues. Selwyn Hughes, who founded CWR in the 1960s, developed the model based on the work of Larry Crabb in the USA. I will attempt to review the model in the light of current theological and counselling sensibilities, and with significant reference to the work of both Hughes and Crabb.

In this book, theological evaluations predominate over practical issues (the former providing the basis for the latter). A fifty-fifty split is not intended.

Such weighting highlights a core theme within this book – that biblical theology is foundational in informing us as to how we might help others.

I have aimed therefore at discussing biblical themes with a primary focus on how they can shape our understanding of people, specifically where this impacts the way Christians might help people through their problems. The Waverley Model's theological presuppositions are given some historical perspective. However, because of the contemporary focus of my book, this is not intended to be exhaustive.

The evaluative framework utilised in this book has itself been used by Jones and Butman to articulate elements that constitute a counselling model. Both the Association of Christian Counsellors (ACC) and the British Association for Counselling and Psychotherapy (BACP) require prospective accrediting counsellors to demonstrate a coherence of theory and practice that make relevant Jones and Butman's criteria within both secular and Christian counselling institutions. We will look at what questions need to be asked, and subsequently answered, in order to provide a model with internal and external (theological and practical) coherence and cogency.

Framework for evaluating the Waverley Model of Counselling

In their evaluative framework, Jones and Butman suggest that all counselling models (secular and Christian) need to include five basic elements in order to operate coherently and be open to critical scrutiny. These elements are:

- Philosophical assumptions

- A model of personality

- A model of health

- A model of abnormality

- A model of psychotherapy.

Whilst not all will agree precisely with these elements, Jones and Butman's framework has been explicitly supported by other leading voices in this field, such as McMinn and Campbell. Jones and Butman also cite Robert Roberts as having independently identified evaluating criteria similar to theirs. From a secular perspective, Horton affirms the evaluative framework used in this book as broadly correlating with empirical research findings with regard to important issues which need to be addressed when constructing a counselling model. It can also be seen that the evaluative framework used in this book covers four spiritual/existential questions, which Baucham asserts are basic to human consciousness across all times and cultures: Who am I? (model of personality); Why am I here? (model of health – in so far as this carries implicit assumptions regarding 'the good life', or that which ultimately makes us happy); What is wrong with the world? (model of abnormality); How can what is wrong be made right? (model of psychotherapy). The first category (philosophical assumptions) is not included as it constitutes the basis of knowledge through which the other categories are addressed.

The following is a brief outline of Jones and Butman's framework by way of introduction; further elaboration will be found in the rest of the book. This outline will describe the criteria, giving some illustration of issues raised by reference to other approaches.

Philosophical Assumptions

Basic presuppositions about truth, reality and people offer a starting point for enquiry and act as foundations upon which counselling and pastoral care rest. Our basic beliefs or world-view provide stories out of which we may proceed to answer universal human questions such as: Who are we? Where are we? What is wrong? What is the solution? It therefore follows that a therapist's foundational beliefs shape which therapeutic concepts and related practical interventions are utilised.

As well as providing a starting point, philosophical assumptions also help establish ideas regarding the end point of counselling, on the grounds that foundational beliefs give rise to ideas regarding what is practically desirable and realistic, and hence what direction and form therapy might take. Chapter 1 discusses four central issues which comprise 'starting points' for the Waverley Model of Counselling:

1. Authority and sufficiency of Scripture

2. Relating theology and psychology

3. Sin

4. The image of God.

The Waverley Model's perspectives will be set alongside the views of others, suggesting implications for the counselling process.

Model of Personality

Jones and Butman use the term 'model of personality' to denote beliefs about how people develop, ie what sort of factors shape personal growth and which ones may be considered central or peripheral in that process. Such factors could include, for example: biological, cultural, spiritual, role modelling, the effects of sin and the Holy Spirit's participation in changes which promote health.

Beyond the above points, Jones and Butman outline an issue that needs to be borne in mind when exploring this general area, and which is of practical importance: Is the model of personality clear, yet at the same time still comprehensive? Grenz understands theology's task as portraying Christian belief in a comprehensive and coherent manner, and to relate those beliefs in an accurate way to today's culture. In light of this statement, a theologically rooted model should meet these requirements of clarity but not at the expense of being incomprehensive. Clarity may be achieved at the expense of simplicity. In such circumstances, the counsellee(s) could expect too much too soon, leading to frustration and despair. Alternatively, comprehensiveness may be obtained at the cost of such opaqueness that it is not accessible and hence of no practical value. Can the model embrace diversity (eg gender, culture and race)? This question alludes again to the issue of relevance, yet on this occasion focuses on how the vast array of human conditions and experiences may be accounted for. A holistic theory of personality will incorporate elements such as the physical and spiritual, ie relationships between aspects of ourselves and those between us and others.

Chapter 2 examines the Waverley Model of Counselling in an attempt to locate its theory of personality within the varied spectrum of other historical and contemporary models (eg historically its correlation with Augustine's ideas; contemporarily with Crabb's work). The implications for counselling will then be discussed.

Model of Health

The model of health refers to how a model defines normal or healthy functioning. If the shaping factors are optimal, what should a healthy human being look like? A vision of normal humanity will be constructed, either explicitly or implicitly and an account of motivation and personality structure will be offered. For instance, Freud believed that unconscious biological drives (especially sex) were at the root of motivation, whereas Adler saw a mastery over our world as the prime human motive. Alternatively, Fairbairn regarded relationship to others as the primary motive. Bowlby, on the other hand, whilst highlighting relationship with others, viewed its importance as an outworking of an evolutionary process in which the survival of one's genes was a primary goal. Other theories have also been proposed emerging from humanistic and cognitive perspectives.

McMinn and Campbell contrast their integrative model's view of motivation with motivational theories underpinning cognitive therapy, believing that their view gives an adequate insight into the range of human experience.

Chapter 3 outlines the Waverley Model's perspective on this issue and places this within a broader historical and biblical account. This includes a discussion of the ramifications for the counselling process.

Model of Abnormality

The model of abnormality covers questions regarding what goes wrong when normal development is hindered. Specific models will develop a certain 'picture' of abnormality, along with its related impact upon the individual and others around them. Representing a Christian world-view, Jones and Butman assert that we will want to know whether Christian virtues are viewed as abnormal, for example, faith in God, obedience and accountability to God. Faw points out that the terms 'normal' and 'abnormal' can be viewed from two basic perspectives. One describes 'what is', the other describes 'what ought to be'. The former denotes a statistical definition regarding what commonly occurs; the latter is an ethical judgment, which provides the basis for denoting normal or abnormal, whether or not it is popularly occurring.

Faw helpfully points out that for evangelical Christians in particular, Jesus Christ is the model of normality (ie fully functioning human) and this provides an objective criterion against which abnormality may be defined. A focus on Christ in this manner stands in contrast to prevalent secular views, for example, Rogers, where self-reference is valued – no objective criterion is offered.

In cognitive therapy it is acknowledged that the therapist may act as a 'healthy' role model, but this is not, in practice, applied to Christ in any way. At best, Christ theoretically could be used as normative, but only on a pragmatic basis (if deemed adaptive) rather than as a central definition out of principle. For Christians, as Christ is the image of God (Col. 1:15; Heb. 1:3) and full humanity was created in this image, to model Christ is synonymous with a movement away from abnormality. This is because Christ is the prototype of humanity before creation – Christ precedes Adam.

In relation to our personal responsibility for pathological outcomes, the question could be asked as to whether causation is viewed as balancing individual and systemic factors. Various models will give more or less (or an absolute) emphasis to one or other of these dimensions. Adams, for instance, emphasises individual factors (personal sin and organic illness) as the agents of abnormality. There are a variety of well-known approaches that span this continuum, including humanistic psychology, psychoanalysis and behavioural approaches.

Chapter 4 identifies the Waverley Model's perspective on this issue and shows how Jesus is portrayed as a model of normality, based on an evangelical view of Scripture as God's revealed truth.

Model of Psychotherapy

The model of psychotherapy (or counselling) refers to how an individual or group may go about helping others to restore or establish healthy functioning. This implies an overall goal towards which the counselling process is orientated. Techniques proposed in fostering the above goal will need to be moral and ethical, and counselling may be seen more as a catalyst to 'real change', which could occur, for example, in church, family and work contexts. Given the importance that the Holy Spirit plays in Scripture regarding positive change, a particularly evangelical Christian approach will need to account for what part the Spirit might be expected to take in the therapeutic process. The Waverley Model is centred on the importance of turning to Christ in order to 'turn our lives around' and affect real and long-lasting change.

Chapter 5 will explain how this process is articulated, and discuss what this might look like in the counselling endeavour, and its implications when working with non-Christians.

Chapter 1

Philosophical Assumptions

Authority and sufficiency of Scripture

The Waverley Model's stance on the authority and sufficiency of Scripture is given great significance in its approach to counselling, and so is worth exploring in detail. With reference to 2 Peter 1:20, an appeal is made by extension to all Scripture having its origin in God to ascertain the supremacy of Scripture as the ultimate test of truth against which all non-biblical ideas must be judged. Although a monochrome view of Scripture's function as authoritative truth (as will be shown) needs to be guarded against, the divine origin of Scripture is a key issue that affects if and how Scripture is used in counselling. This also applies to conceptions of salvation.

The relative clarity of Scripture is ultimately a position of faith warranted by a belief in God as a clear communicator of His Word in conjunction with the purpose for which it was given. While debating various perspectives on inerrancy, Hurding helpfully expresses that 'God is able to mediate the Bible's essential reliability to us today in spite of the presence of various textual errors.'[4] Marshall asserts that both sides of the debate believe 'in the entire trustworthiness of Scripture for its God-given purpose'.[5]

The Waverley Model's approach is challenged by those who have an awareness that the different genres in Scripture require a varied interpretive stance. Schnabel offers a model where the assertive prophetic paradigm is but one of four types. The prophetic is deemed to require obedience, implying an authoritative directedness. Other genres, for example wisdom literature, require observance. Hopeful trust, for example, in God's promises to the faithful, invites us to identify with another's experience, as in the Psalms and Song of Songs. The Parables in Scripture contain riddles and Ecclesiastes contains questions, which by their nature cannot be obeyed. Therefore, Scripture as a dispenser of dogma is but one of its varied modes of communication; it is thus unhelpful to subsume all of Scripture under a prophetic paradigm.

The Waverley Model uses 1 Peter 1:25 to assert the difference between transient human-based theories of human functioning as opposed to that found in the 'eternal word of God'.[6] Alternatively, Ward gives human wisdom a more authoritative role in relation to Scripture. Grenz and Franke also deny a notion of Scripture as either 'downloaded' from God or neutral. Instead they argue it is always culturally embedded and thus to some extent contextually derived. Additionally, with regards to the issue of human authority, Ward endorses the principle of the Church being given 'the keys of the kingdom' (Matt. 16:19; 18:18) as evidence that the Church is endowed with power to interpret the essentials of faith – a dialogue process rather than a top down, one-way communication where the Church passively receives the given truth. Ward points out that the Church decided the canon of Scripture and thus the canon is viewed in a more open-ended manner – it could be 'built on and extended and complemented by subsequent human experience'.[7] This stance gives most room for the use of scientific data in formulating our basic beliefs. It does not, of necessity, hold Scripture as the final authority and so begs the question as to where final authority lies.

Hughes, on the other hand, affirms a 'high view' of Scripture, stating that, 'I believe the Bible, in its original form, to be divinely inspired and without error in all its parts.'[8] As a result, Hughes considers the Bible to be a central source for helping people with personal problems. In saying this, he does not offer an account of how our humanity interacts with the divine revelation of Scripture. This absence leaves Hughes open to the criticism of what Malley terms a 'folk hermeneutic' – the idea that biblical texts have objective and independent meanings, and the reader's task is to obtain this objectively. Given our cultural contexts we can question a seemingly enlightenment based notion of interpretive certainty; we can agree with Carson who asserts, 'All of us see things only in part, and never without some measure of distortion.'[9] Such awareness of our limits need not bankrupt our faith as if we cannot know anything; rather, our awareness of limits might be the context in which humility could flourish amidst the stands that we make, ie openness to others' views so that we do not claim the interpretive 'high ground'.

Hughes advocates the use of Scripture as a sign that we appreciate its ultimate authority. This may be true, but the converse does not necessarily follow, as numerous other factors impact on the use of Scripture, for example: the context of the counselling practice; the nature of the issues being worked upon; and the stage of the counselling process. Crabb, from whom Hughes developed his model, has a similar 'high view' of Scripture, asserting that the Bible provides a framework through which we may view every counselling-related problem. This would follow if we assume 'framework' is synonymous with 'world-view', and that this in turn has some direct relevance for every problem.

Regarding sufficiency, the Waverley Model teaches that the Bible enables us to 'find a frame of reference for understanding the causes for all non-organic psychological problems and the resources with which to deal with them'.[10] It can be argued that such a stance rests upon a notion of salvation that includes potential transformative power to overcome our problems of living, out of which contexts people may seek counselling help.

In this context, the issue of sufficiency relates to a debate regarding the degree to which the Bible alone is adequate to explain and help resolve relevant issues. In relation to this, Weeks poses two helpful questions which provide a means of exploring the relevance of concepts of salvation and their relationship with healthy 'successful' living: Does the Bible claim authority? Does the Bible have the character of an authoritative source?

Regarding the first question, we may note 2 Timothy 3:15–17, where Paul asserts that 'all Scripture' being 'God breathed' 'thoroughly equips' us for 'every good work'. Weeks observes that 'every good work' is rather imprecise. Does it refer to religious work only? If so, does this include the kind of issues with which people present in counselling? Looking at 'every good work' within its co-text we might conclude that Paul's implied domain relating to 'every' is salvation (v15) and righteousness (v16), ie sanctification. If this interpretation is accurate, it still begs the question as to whether what in our contemporary culture we might refer to as mental health issues are subsumed by Paul's use of the terms 'salvation' and 'right living'.

McGrath, using the existential language of Martin Heidegger, poses two categories of being for all humans. Inauthentic existence equates to alienation from our 'true self' and destiny, and is rooted in sin (separation from God). Authentic existence (being in relationship with God) enables people to achieve (or at least make progress towards) their full potential. Considering the pastoral consequences of these terms, McGrath admits that the Greek verb *sozein* (to save) is notoriously difficult to translate. However, interestingly enough for our discussion, McGrath states that this is because it is such a broad concept, including physical and spiritual healing (Mark 5:28; Luke 7:50; 9:24) defined as in harmonious relationship with God, self, others and the environment. McGrath asserts a fundamental link between 'health', 'wholeness' and 'salvation'. MacNutt has a 'Catholic perspective' and takes a similar view, where what may be referred to as psychopathology is subsumed by the term 'sin'; the antidote is salvation. Backus, who represents a reformed perspective, argues similarly. If these views are valid, then the Bible can be claimed as a relevant authority for helping people with counselling issues.

Fenton rightly points out that throughout church history the doctrine of salvation has been understood in a variety of ways, and its meaning has been much disputed. He further notes that different human contributors who together make up the canon of Scripture also use the term to mean different things. In arguing for theological unity amidst diverse biblical usage of the term salvation, Holmes picks out 'being in Christ' and 'eschatological (end times) fullness' as overarching themes. Subsumed within these themes he includes personal, social and environmental transformation. More specifically he writes:

> *In the Pauline Corpus, salvation is understood as what God has done through Christ, and particularly his death and resurrection, to bring about deliverance from sin and death, wholeness, health, moral and physical transformation, and enduring new life.*[11]

Transformations which include the above dimensions have the possibility, at least in part, of being realised in the 'here and now', whilst only fully experienced eschatologically, and so a theological foundation for the relevance of Scripture within counselling can be supported. This point is of a broadly principled nature, and does not offer in itself a methodology of Scriptural application. Additionally, it should be noted that the biblical witness also includes wisdom literature (see Chapter 3 'Repentance and Wisdom'), which points towards authority beyond itself, eg science and human experience. This avoids a crude correlation between 'getting saved' and being made whole in so far as wisdom points to a lifelong process of learning, including from sources beyond Scripture in order to become mature. In this broad sense, one might 'be saved' but not be wise, and so still not mature to 'life in all its fullness'.

These broad understandings of salvation form the foundation of hope for change with which we enter the counselling process, although precise predictions of when and how an individual may enter into any aspect of their salvation cannot be assumed.

Regarding Weeks' second question, 'Does the Bible have the character of an authoritative source?' he argues that the Bible may be deemed sufficient if it is either comprehensive in the relevant domain, or if it provides foundational principles from which detail may be deduced.

The Waverley Model's position is based on Weeks' second point that the Bible offers foundational principles:

> *If we understand the Bible sufficiently, we will find a frame*
> *of reference for understanding the causes for all non-organic*
> *psychological problems and the resources with which to deal*
> *with them.*[12]

Crabb also concurs with this position, viewing it as a crucial premise of his model. Crabb's later writings also echo a similar theme. Further supporting evidence from the Waverley Model Trainers' Notes include: 'We believe that God has revealed the truth about the essential nature of Himself and the nature of man in the Bible.'[13] In the context of this discussion the phrase 'essential nature' stands out as emphasising the Bible's central, if not exclusive, role.

Adams' belief that the Bible alone is sufficient for helping people appears not to be supported by Scripture itself. Wright notes that it points away from itself to other sources of God's authority (creation Psa. 19, and human observations – 'wisdom'). Crabb himself appeals for such openness. Hurding, like Wright, argues for a broader understanding of how Scriptural truth may be applied to the counselling process beyond the prophetic (information from God) paradigm. He places the prophetic amongst other biblical ministries such as the wise healer (therapeutic insight); the pastoral (relational emphasis); and the priestly (spiritual direction). All of these paradigms can be given space within counselling to work out their particular understanding of Scripture. The implication of the above is that Adams' position of the Bible alone being sufficient, ironically turns out not to be fully biblical, ie it reduces the broader authority outlined within the canon back to the canon itself. The broader understanding of Scripture's function, which Hurding and others state gives credence to the potential healing power of relationships (Hurding's pastoral domain) and human insight (wisdom) alongside that of Scripture. As Thiselton points out, God's commission for humanity to do good may include the direct use of biblical insight, but is understood much more generally, ie with whatever we have at our disposal which may benefit others, for instance, specific skills or experiences.

Summary and evaluation

We have explored how Hughes takes a 'high view' of Scripture and regards it as a central source for helping people with counselling-related problems. For Hughes, the Bible plays a central role in counselling because he believes that Scripture is divinely inspired and consequently, for him, is fully authoritative and without error. Hughes' opinion as to Scripture's dual purpose of informing us of sound doctrine and transforming the heart, sits well with traditional evangelicalism. It is less clear whether Hughes' view on inerrancy has always occupied the centre ground of evangelical orthodoxy. We looked at a more liberal perspective proposed by Ward, who gives greater weight to the human aspect of the production of Scripture. This carries a more 'open ended' view of God's truth, which could be expanded and developed beyond Scripture because God gives humans 'the keys of the kingdom'. This principle has a bearing upon ideas regarding integration of biblically-based theology with scientifically-based psychology, which is discussed in the next section.

It was also noted that Crabb adopts an approach similar to Hughes, believing the Bible offers a framework of truths through which we can approach all non-organically caused problems. Crabb argues for his position by contrasting God's eternal truths in Scripture with transient human wisdom. I have argued that Weeks' questions make the issue clearer when he asserts that the Bible equips us for 'every good work', though he does state that this phrase is hard to interpret precisely. Similarly, in speaking of salvation, McGrath argues for a broad interpretation, which allows us to expect that Scripture will offer profoundly relevant insights into personal problems of everyday living, of the type that cause people to require counselling, for example, guilt, anger, fear, identity issues and the need for love. This perspective on salvation was also shared by MacNutt and Backus, representing a Catholic and Reformed perspective respectively.

Dismissing biblical authority on the grounds that it is not exhaustive assumes that other books are exhaustive. How can any book on any subject say everything? A more helpful approach in denoting authority is to investigate to what extent a book says important and relevant things and/or claims authority for itself. This is explored in the following chapter. Lastly, in accepting that the production of Scripture is the outcome of a divine-human partnership, this in no way need undermine our confidence in its truthfulness. Packer states the issue succinctly:

> *It was no more necessary that the Bible, being human, should be wrong sometimes than it was for Jesus, being human, to go astray in conduct or teaching. Those who confess a sinless Christ cannot consistently dismiss this analogous belief in an inerrant Bible.*[14]

Having said this, in taking the human element seriously regarding the production of Scripture, any model must engage with the historical and cultural contexts of the human writers, and how these issues shaped the ideas conveyed and the words used.

When applying Scripture to the counselling situation, it can be recognised that Scripture was not primarily intended to be a counselling manual! As such, it is important to make explicit a methodology which gives a rationale as to why certain aspects of Scripture are used as opposed to others. Hughes is not clear regarding the reason for his starting place as compared to other possibilities. Additionally, it would also be helpful to make clear one's interpretive approach to any text used, but again, Hughes is not explicit about his method in this regard. This may be a function of the popular level at which he writes, but it does weaken his case when scrutinised at an academic level as the above important issues are foundational aspects which inform counselling methodology.

Relating theology and psychology

In order to provide a pragmatic organising structure to this section, four differing views on integration will be outlined, compared and critiqued. Each view is to be found within the book, Psychology *and* Christian*ity: Four Views*, edited by Johnson and Jones. These views are in turn articulated by four 'major voices' in this field as evidenced by their academic backgrounds, longevity of involvement and various major honours and posts held within the psychology, counselling and theology professions. A second reason for this book's usefulness is its deliberate dialogical structure in which each contributor critiques the other three, thus clarifying similarities and differences between the approaches.

With one exception (Roberts), it parallels and builds upon Kirwan's previous ideas regarding four approaches to integration, which are as follows:

1. The 'unchristian approach' sees no contribution from theology to psychology when formulating therapy. Psychology is viewed as fundamental and comprehensive – no need for divine revelation.

2. The 'spiritualised approach' takes an opposite stance, and believes that the Bible alone is needed as a basis in formulating therapy – psychology is irrelevant at best, at worst it is harmful as it contains 'truths' that compete with the Bible, and can thus lead to heretical ideas and practises.

3. The 'parallel approach' regards both disciplines as relevant. Yet both are kept separate because the Bible's theology is seen as showing us the way of salvation, not the way of psychology; scientific and religious ideas are viewed as mutually exclusive.

4. The 'integrated approach' assumes both disciplines are ultimately true as God is the God of both reason and revelation. Reason (in this context derived via research) is seen as a Godly endeavour as it helps humans to fulfil God's mandate to subdue the earth and master it.

In *Four Views*, there is a more advanced exposition on the various ways in which the two disciplines of Christian theology and scientific psychology 'sit together'. In their introductory chapter, under the heading, 'Issues that Distinguish Christian Approaches to Psychology', Johnson and Jones suggest that the main issue at stake is the validity given to varied sources of psychological knowledge, empirical research, Scripture and theology, philosophy and history. More specifically, two subsidiary questions are posed: 'Is the Bible relevant to counselling?' and 'To what extent should the Bible's teachings have a controlling influence on counselling theory, research and practice?' Unsurprisingly, we return to issues of authority (it is necessary to be relevant to stand a chance of being authoritative) and sufficiency.

In *Four Views* the approaches discussed with their authors are as follows: 'Levels of Explanation View' (LOE) by David Myers; 'Integration View' (I) by Gary Collins; 'Christian Psychology View' (CP) by Robert Roberts; and 'Biblical Counselling View' (BC) by David Powlison.

Levels of Explanation view

The LOE view considers the two disciplines of theology and psychology as representing two different domains. As such, 'theology and psychology in particular, use different methods of investigation, have different objects of study, and answer different questions'.[15] As a Christian, who is a psychologist, Myers regards the ultimate purpose of both disciplines to be identical. He cites major scientists through history, such as Pascal, Bacon and Newton who, having a Christian faith, regarded any scientific exploration of God's universe as an act of worship. Thus, Myers argues that, 'Disciplined rigorous inquiry is part of what it means to love God with our minds.'[16] This is true regarding the potential motivation of any individual scientist who shares a Christian world-view, and applies the commission in Genesis 1:26 'to rule' as being fulfilled amongst other things, through the endeavours of science. However, this stance is not an argument for the integration (or not) of scientific findings and biblical truths in general. In addition, Myers does perceive some overlap between the two disciplines, arguing that psychological research can complement Christian belief. This sits well with the Waverley Model's perspective and biblically gives credence to a wisdom interpretive method, seeing the Spirit at work in some secular activities including scientific investigation. Such a perspective is laudable as it does not marginalise theology, but keeps doctrines such as imago Dei and creation as foundational tools for grappling with the human condition in general, from which vantage point scientific enquiry may fill in detail. Myers' view, at the same time, appears to limit the impact of salvation to our spirits, as this is regarded as a separate domain to our psyches (our minds). However, where overlap is acknowledged, data from psychology is used to elucidate theological themes. For example, existentialism's view of angst and Freud's work on defence mechanisms and basic anxiety articulate our propensity to prefer comforting untruths rather than uncomfortable reality. This can be one way of illuminating the Christian doctrine of original sin because in this doctrine it is not assumed that we start life normally neutral or inherently inclined to pursue truth at all costs.

At the same time, it is necessary to acknowledge the increasing awareness of the provisional and approximate nature of scientific data, rather than adopt a naïve positivist stance that science simply discovers reality. Modern physics is a good case in point, where the universality of phenomena is difficult to assert. This theme is part of a broader critique of universal certainty: post-modernity. Grenz and Franke define the term as one which 'implies the rejection of certain central features of the modern project, such as its quest for certain, objective, and universal knowledge'.[17]

Moltmann concludes:

> *Scientific theories can no longer present themselves as being identical with the world as it really is. These theories are models – that is to say, observations within the limits set by the experiments.*[18]

Myers' perspective closely matches that of the parallel approach in Kirwan's book. One corollary that follows from a starting premise of separate domains is that any issue of conflict will be concluded through a debate regarding its location in either field of inquiry. For example, Collins (I) criticises Myers' assertion that homosexuality must be accepted if research proves it is a genetic inclination and not a chosen sexual disposition. Myers' reasoning would follow only if research is afforded final authority to define the nature of reality. For Collins, this debate raises the fundamental issue of authority, an issue which he rightly considers as 'core':

> *In this book the core issue is whether the Bible is the authoritative Word of God that transforms and becomes standard against which we evaluate our psychology or whether psychological science is the standard against which we evaluate our beliefs?*[19]

This reasoning assumes one body of knowledge 'stands alone' and subsumes the other, whereas Roberts argues for a rather more dynamic understanding of how two disciplines can relate. One will predominate (the system) over the other (the element added to the system), but both will in some way be changed by their interaction.

Integration view

Collins (I) believes attempts at integration are worthwhile because they engage our faith with people in the world for whom we have a responsibility – the 'Great Commission' in Matthew 28. Integration for Collins is a way of attempting to understand the world of the Word and works of God; that is 'one's grasp of the truth, finite and faltering as it is, will be enhanced by bringing these sources of truth together'.[20] However, if Roberts' dynamic understanding is correct, both will be changed, but not of necessity enriched – the contact could in principle be detrimental, ie Adams and the Bobgans' fear of Scripture being 'watered down'. Collins regards the Bible as containing rich data concerning humanity, whilst not having been written as a psychological textbook. He does however agree with Van Leeuwen in believing that the Bible provides critical background assumptions which give us a framework against which we may judge psychological theories. This belief concurs with Hughes' and Crabb's positions. Examples of these assumptions include the role of sin in shaping behaviour; the reason why temptations are so powerful; and the role of the Holy Spirit in healing.

Christian psychology view

Roberts points out that integration occurs when an element is combined with a system. He then asks whether psychology or the Bible is the system, ie which is added to which? For Roberts it is clear that we integrate psychological insights into Christian thought and practice, and that these are rooted in the Bible's standards. Roberts summarises his view: 'The process of integration will result in a state of integration that will be the psychologically informed Christian thought and practice of a given community at a given time.'[21]

Roberts' (CP) view on integration turns upon our understanding of what is psychology. Citing Van Leeuwen, Roberts takes a broader historical perspective to challenge the current psychological establishment's view of what constitutes psychology. Roberts refers to a range of authors, from the ancient Greeks to modern writers such as Dickens and C.S. Lewis, describing their works as 'sources of tremendous psychological insight into issues of human motivation, basic psychological needs, forms and sources of pathology and much more'.[22] Roberts thus supports a broader knowledge base than scientific psychology would permit, and so grants authority to these, and other such works, ie carrying out formal empirical research and/ or training as a psychologist is not seen as the only route to obtain essential psychological knowledge.

Roberts gives numerous examples of such works including Augustine's 'Confessions', seen as embracing the idea that the love and service of God are crucial elements in fostering psychological wellbeing. As such, Roberts uses a broad definition of psychology as 'a coherent body of thought and practice (a system) at least partially articulate for understanding, measuring, assessing and possibly changing peoples' emotions, thoughts, perceptions and behaviours and their dispositions to these'.[23] He negates the view that psychology is defined by one specific method, namely that of the natural sciences. In so doing, his critique concurs with an existential challenge to a traditional definition. Indeed, Richardson sees this method as relatively impoverished when studying humans as it forces us to take an objective 'spectator' position. Furthermore, he appears to doubt whether objectivity is truly obtainable, especially when the field of study (people) is so value laden. This supposed neutrality is seen as denying inevitable moral allegiances and political stances. Using a broad definition of what psychology as a science could include, Roberts wants us to regard Augustine, Baxter, Kierkegaard and others like them as psychologists of primary importance and not as irrelevant at worst, or at best, peripheral to the 'main event' – 'real psychology'.

In a nutshell, Roberts regards the psychological thought and practice of the above historical theologians as a part of their faith, not something separate. Such a stance makes the idea of integration a non-starter; rather, he understands these 'theologians' as teaching a distinctively Christian psychology, which in turn defines our main task as retrieval of these insights and their 'translation' in order to communicate them to the modern contemporary context. A significant example, which may illustrate Robert's emphasis, is the use of the term 'sin', which has decreased as a way of articulating human misery and dysfunction.

Biblical Counselling View

Powlison's (BC) view takes a somewhat antagonistic stance regarding how psychology and Christian theology might relate together. They are believed to represent competing philosophies and personality theories. Of the latter, Powlison refers to them as 'alternative spiritualities' which use 'rival' words to describe some of the same phenomenon. Regarding human nature, neuroses is a word which Powlison believes is used to denote the biblical concept of 'lusts of the flesh'. Such practical matters arise from the different world-views held by the two disciplines. Powlison believes psychology to be seriously impoverished by the fact that it is embedded within a secular ideological frame of reference. He states:

> *In a God-made, God-sustained, God-interpreted world,*
> *observational data will express the distorting effect of the*
> *secularity in any theory. Observations are always presented in*
> *a context of meanings, beliefs, values, priorities and goals.*[24]

This stance echoes that emphasised earlier by Johnson, Kirwan and Vitz asserting that all intellectual activity is 'kingdom' activity. It contrasts with an epistemological stance which assumes that knowing reality can be (with some care) simply observed. Powlison gives the example from Scripture of Peter and the Pharisees, who observed Jesus with the same tools (ears, eyes and reason) and yet drew totally different conclusions.

Summary and evaluation

Myers' (LOE) view pointed out that rigorous enquiry could be part of what it means to love God with your entire mind. Such a perspective is consistent with biblical ethics, since it is also part of God's commission from Genesis 1 to have dominion (for more detail see 'Image as Functional' later in this chapter). Myers argued that, historically major scientists such as Bacon, Newton and Pascal, saw their work in this regard as an act of worship and as a contemporary voice. Myers views his own endeavours in a similar vein.

However, Myers does not give significant weight to the distorting power of values, political allegiances and ideology, which in modern psychology are overwhelmingly secular. This is the principle which Powlison's (BC) view advocates. We need not assume all findings are thus distorted, but that the degree of distortion (if any) will differ depending on the 'psychological' domain of interest. For instance, science may be in the best position to explain accurately how emotional or cognitive impairment may follow brain damage from a car accident. Logically, given its traditional empirical basis, Science may not speak with the same authority when constructing models of motivation (personality theory), as this domain is not empirically testable beyond self report with regard to what people think motivates them. A psychoanalytic and biblical perspective on the human propensity for self-deception may quickly establish that awareness and cause are not necessarily synonymous. Powlison rightly regards modern psychological theories of motivation as 'spiritualities' competing with biblical accounts. Others, like Van Leeuwen, make a valid point in questioning the relevance of an approach emphasising objectivity, where the 'objects' of study are actually 'subjects', and whose essence could be regarded as highly value laden. Therefore, it is right to conclude that humans are of a different quality or 'substance' to that of the objects studied in the 'hard' sciences, and thus require different methods of investigation rooted in different sources of knowledge. This criticism of supposedly neutral knowledge is summarised by Vitz, 'The single greatest cultural contribution of post modernity is that it eliminates the presumption of intellectual neutrality that modernity automatically associated with sceptical rationalism.'[25] Both Kirwan and Johnson also make similar critiques of objectivity, the latter using the biblical concept of 'kingdom' to assert that all knowledge is gained via a spiritually charged enterprise. Collins, on the other hand, argues that we will be enriched by integrating insights from both disciplines, but that theology based on Scripture will provide critical assumptions against which psychological truth must be tested. In this manner he mirrors Hughes and Crabb. This latter issue was clarified by Roberts' discussion of integration where Roberts argues that apart from a synthesis, where two things are equally wedded together, integration occurs when an element is added to a system. For our focus this faces us with the issue of whether psychology or theology is our system. Roberts, like Collins, Crabb and Hughes, is clear that our system is based on Scripture, Christian thought and practice. This is how practically they work out the notion of keeping Scripture 'central'.

Roberts' (CP) approach helps us to question the establishment's definition of psychology as a method (science) and so opens the way for a broader historical/theological perspective concerning who may be considered psychologists of primary importance. Roberts offers a laudable challenge which seeks to retrieve the insights of thinkers of distinctively Christian psychology and translate them into our modern language. To illustrate Roberts' point, it is worth noting how Christian Counselling students are familiar with the works of Rogers and Freud, but are not always critically aware of their particular anti-Christian bias, and how this impacts their ideas. These students may dismiss the likes of Aquinas and Augustine as being unscientific, pre-modern and non-psychologists, and thereby cast away rich treasures of biblically informed psychological work. This very process can be explained through Johnson's notion of all intellectual authority being 'kingdom work' and thus spiritually and epistemologically 'charged'. Thus Roberts, Crabb and Hughes' approaches to integration are valid – a truly Christian approach must presume the relevance of, and be centred on the foundational ideas of the Bible, and of Christians down the ages, who have sought to apply its distinctive perspective. The notion of sin, which is the subject of the next section, is a good example of how the 'kingdom struggle' regarding concepts and use of distinctively Christian ideas and language, translates to counselling theory and practice. Based on this stance, we are not free to dismiss the concept of sin as outmoded, even if in our general culture and some of our churches, such language and concepts are increasingly avoided.

Sin

As Anderson notes, there is no universal consensus regarding the definition of sin; this is partly a result of the variety of words used to describe sin in Scripture. This fact supports an approach to thinking about sin in a manner that does not reduce the concept to one image or tradition. Erickson delineates a progression of the concept of sin from the Old to the New Testament, from outward acts or 'sins', to inner disposition. Citing Galatians 5, Erickson perceives Paul, like Jesus, as also emphasising the disposition behind the sins. Collins also regards sin as an issue relevant to the core of our humanity. 'The Bible presents sin as an inner force, an inherent condition, a controlling power that lies at the core of our being.'[26] Such a stance helps avoid a view of sin as superficial, and thus an insignificant description when articulating pathology. However, this stance might be helpfully balanced with a clear grasp of sin, not as ultimately ontological, but as a 'parasite', a 'deprivation of good' taught by the Church fathers. Collins further notes the implications for counselling, for if humankind is seen as good or neutral, problems must logically be located in the environment. Having defined sin as inherent and 'core', Collins does show a broad view as to its location and function. Firstly, he regards sin as personal acts of rebellion (Psa. 51:2,4; Rom. 1:32; 5:14); secondly, as an attitude (Matt. 5:28; Rom. 12:19; Heb. 12:15); thirdly, as a force as in Paul's struggle with the 'inner law of sin' (Rom. 7:23–27; 8:2); and fourthly, a state that we all inherit because of Adam's sin (Rom. 5:12–19; Eph. 2:1–3). Jones and Butman also describe sin in terms of all these categories; a state of being as well as acts or thoughts, but also a power that holds us in bondage. In a brief survey of differing views regarding the nature of sin, Jones and Butman characterise the 'classic reformed view' as a rebellious refusal to believe God and thus a breaking of His law. Whilst acknowledging many other understandings of the nature of sin, Jones and Butman contrast the reformed view with that of Niebuhr and Tillich where sin arises out of the tension between dependence and our free nature, which yields an unwillingness to be dominated or to be held responsible. A postmodern theme is that of humanity 'as victim of a force beyond its control'.[27] Bultmann relates the bondage of sin to an inevitable outworking of processes wrought from an inauthentic self-striving that captures us in the actions of the past. Freedom is for him a gift of the Spirit that enables us to be instead determined by the future. In the helpful spirit of anti-reductionism, Jones and Butman offer their own view as incorporating both reformed and existential perspectives as complementary, ie sin as a violation of law and relationship; as individual and corporate; rebellion and anxiety; in bondage to and yet responsible for.

Plantinga expresses a similar view when defining sin as not only a breaking of the law, but of the covenant with 'the Saviour'; it is 'shalom-breaking', personal as well as legal. Like Erickson and Jones and Butman, Plantinga perceives sin as both an act and a disposition. Others also see acts of sin emerging from a primary disposition: 'The heart (the seat of thought and action) is assumed to be wicked and constantly producing evil, (Gen. 6:5; cf. 8:21; Jer. 17:9; Matt. 15:19).'[28] Both Jesus and Paul viewed sin as an internal power, not merely external acts. Under a section on the extent and depth of sin, Erickson highlights the use of the Hebrew verb *chashab* (used 180 times), which expresses the tendency of the heart to plan and devise evil.

Depravity

Having highlighted the primacy given to humanity in God's creation order and the assertion that people are made in God's image, the Waverley Model Trainers' Notes use the language of depravity to discuss the consequences of the Fall. This depravity is taught as affecting all areas of human functioning, indicating an alignment with the Reformed doctrine of total depravity. Whilst this doctrine states that no area is unaffected by sin, it does not imply that humans are incapable of doing good things. Rather the deep-rooted and pervasive nature of sin shapes life, to use Paul's language (Rom. 7:7–25) it enslaves us and dictates the direction of life. As 'total' denotes that the entire person is involved rather than just some parts, this 'strong' view of sin points the way towards the necessity for a radical solution. Without this stance, sin becomes a verb rather than a noun, ie something we do rather than an essential description. As such, it promotes a search for the cause of sin as an external force, for an essentially sinless being would not act sinfully unless an external element(s) were distorting the true nature. The Reformed stance (sin as an essential description) can lead to the opposite danger of assuming all sin stems only from individual corruption. Each view can be regarded as a form of reductionism – social or individual. It can be seen that both stances limit a broader biblical picture, and this should be avoided if our doctrine and related practice is to represent a full biblical theology. The Reformed view may be less popular today, as evidenced by changing patterns of liturgical confessions. Thiselton also cites an 'ill-informed' understanding of the doctrine of total depravity as a cause of its popular demise. Furthermore, Pannenberg connects the trend towards a narrow conception of sin as 'acts' to the decline of the doctrine of original sin.

To the extent that all psychological problems are rooted in personal sin, which is encompassed by the above broader definition, then the Waverley Model will give an adequate account of its cause. However, notions of destructive forces damaging to psychological growth residing outside the individual are not emphasised in the initial presentation of the Waverley Model rather, inward corruption and culpability of the individual take centre stage. This is made clear by observing the Waverley Model in diagrammatic form (see Appendix A).

It is worth noting that many of the prominent secular psychological models available to Hughes during the years when the Waverley Model was being formulated also emphasised intra-personal factors when explaining development and so Hughes' model could be read as a 'creature of its time'. Elsewhere, Hughes demonstrates awareness that the consequences of sin are cosmic and not merely residing in our 'inner being'. Hughes concludes his discussion of depravity by stating: 'Inevitably this combination of factors – fallen nature, an environment affected by sin, and a malevolent devil – means that we are surrounded on all sides by temptation.'[29] Having noted the above, the possible implications for helping individuals caught amidst these broad forces is not developed beyond a personal call to repentance. However, Webster distinguishes between a 'broader' and 'tighter' definition of original sin. This allows us to hold in tension individual freedom with its associated culpability for sin, and also external social and/or spiritual forces of sin which each person is born into. Although not responsible for them, each person is profoundly shaped by them. Thus we have a notion of sin that explains why our capacity to resist is undermined. This suggests a shared responsibility, which in principle may vary according to each case in point and may be seen as the individual operating in relation to a context. Speaking of this 'collaboration', McFadyen states, 'The disorder of society and that of culture are also partly responsible for the disorder of desire.'[30] For McFadyen original sin emerges from an essential relatedness not separation.

> *It is 'original' because it is not a phenomenon of our freedom, but the situational dynamics into and through which our wills are born, formed, energised and directed. And yet it is sin, that for which we are held accountable. Guilt is responsibility for the joy of all before the Lord of all.*[31]

For McFadyen, our guilt arises out of our originating dependence on 'the other', a universal matrix of relationality which connects us ultimately to Adam and promotes a self that is open ended and so avoids portrayals of self that are purely individualistic – an essential separateness.

> *If, in the very heart of my 'self,' I am born into radical and intrinsic relationality, for God and others, then one person's sin would be sufficient to disrupt the entire ecology of joy on which my very 'self' depends, for myself to be 'as another'.*[32]

Continuing to conceptualise sin in broad categories, Shields and Bredfelt utilise the often-quoted formula, 'the world, the flesh and the devil'. This formula proves helpful as it, of necessity, leads to explanations that include factors from both inside and outside the individual, with echoes from Genesis that the whole of creation (our contexts) is fallen where 'according to Genesis 3:14–19, nature itself was corrupted by human sin and suffers sin's mournful consequences'.[33] There is, therefore, significant trauma arising from natural external causes such as tsunamis. As well as this, we are also hurt and wounded by moral evil from other human beings; we not only sin and contribute to our own problems, but are 'sinned against' by other people, both individually and collectively. In the light of balancing internal and external causes of sin, McFadyen also helpfully articulates a notion of 'willing' and connected culpability in terms that avoid simple either/or, me or you categorisation. With reference to childhood sexual abuse and the Holocaust, McFadyen states:

> *Willing in these two situations appears bound up with situation.*
> *Description of the pathological dynamics operating here cannot*
> *restrict its attention to acts and to their simple internal causes*
> *(such as free decisions of will).*[34]

McFadyen goes on to suggest abusers should be understood in turn, to some degree, in relation to their contexts, potentially implicating key figures in their development. In turn, the Holocaust needs to be seen not just as a 'German phenomenon', but as one arising out of the whole European history of anti-Semitism; the impact of defeat in World War One; and the conditions imposed which arose out of the armistice, and so on. Amidst such powerful forces, will is seen as 'bent', held captive by, and pulled along by these external forces. This language and conception is an example of what Starkey defines as two of the five categories of sin in Scripture: namely an alien power that holds us captive, and a matrix of evil (a pervasive network of pathological places, situations and people).

For Shields and Bredfelt another aspect of potential pathology arising from a perspective of 'people in context' is their notion of 'world'. This includes the phenomenon which our contemporary culture refers to as stress – demands on a system. In this context it denotes the generic pressures rooted in life outside the security and provision of life in 'The Garden'. Additionally, Shields and Bredfelt point out that suffering and its emotional consequences may arise directly from God. This point is also emphasised by Carson. Firstly, to produce maturity (James 1:2–4; Rom. 5:3–5), secondly, to share in Christ's redemptive suffering (Rom. 8:17), thirdly, as an aspect of God's love, as He disciplines those He loves (Heb. 12:5–11), and fourthly, as a result of divine judgment, (Psa. 98:9; Isa. 33:22). This 'Judgment', whilst fully realised at the end times, has a present facet. As Starkey puts it, 'God judges actions not just at some future time, but even in our present world or personal lives.'[35] Therefore, it can be seen that simply correlating suffering and related pathology with personal sin is too simplistic and reductionist, and does not give adequate weight to contextual factors which have no direct connection to moral culpability, for example stress linked to creaturely limitations, or deep distress arising as we share in Christ's redemptive suffering.

Drawing together the above descriptions of sin's location, we may conclude that if we delineate evil into two categories (moral and natural), the Waverley Model emphasises our own moral evil as the primary cause of our problems. The consequence of this is that it plays down the impact of moral evil done to us by others, and also the impact of natural evil. Within the Waverley Model the impact of natural evil (a post-lapsarian phenomenon) is located within the individual arising from the physical area of functioning. In the introduction to the physical area of functioning, the Waverley Model states: 'Some Christian counsellors show little or no respect for the fact that physical malfunctioning has some influence and impact upon behaviour.'[36] Further elaboration is offered, 'Indeed, some symptoms which appear to be emotionally caused may have their roots in chemical disturbances in the body.'[37] Elsewhere, in *Christ Empowered Living*, a seminal text outlining his ideas, Hughes emphasises the link between Adam's fall and our malfunctioning bodies, 'because of the curse that fell on Adam and Eve, no human body functions perfectly'.[38] It can be seen therefore that the Waverley Model cannot be subsumed under a moral reductionist view of pathology. So viruses can cause depression; allergies influence behaviour; sleep loss can lead to hallucinations. This is a welcomed emphasis, but still needs further development regarding the issue of human weakness beyond that instigated by either the limitations of the body or human culpability alone.

In his article, 'Sin, Weakness and Psychopathology', Johnson takes the debate further regarding the 'dual cause' of potential human misery, arguing that the Bible teaches that sinners create sin and are responsible for it and its effect, and thus repentance is a logical response. On the other hand, weakness or limitation is a given which we are not responsible for, and for which repentance thus has no moral basis. Johnson then articulates a third category, 'moral fault', which combines the above two concepts. Johnson defines moral fault as a weakness in the realm of responsibility. Weakness is viewed as a comparative concept against two measures, either the ideal or the average. Additionally, fault is used in two senses: geological fault (structural), a given weakness that just is; and ethical fault which suggests culpability. Jones and Butman accept Johnson's concept as helpful, but add a third element of developmental weakness they refer to as a type of natural evil. Given Johnson's use of the notion of a continuum, we need to discern the differential contributions of sin and weakness in any given issue where his two categories may apply. This approach helpfully keeps central the notion of persons as agents acting, yet situated in systemic contexts which may enhance or inhibit the ability to choose certain courses of behaviour: humans and their environments are not separable, but intimately involved with each other. In practice, Johnson accepts that this discernment (sin and weakness) may not be easy. He gives three examples: homosexuality, alcoholism and fear. The fear of acknowledging Christ to others is condemned (Matt. 10:32f). However, a weak conscience is not condemned (Rom. 14) as in this context it arises out of a desire to please God and a fear of Him.

Finally, Johnson leaves us in no doubt that the overwhelming emphasis in Scripture is that people are responsible actors, persons, and not objects acted upon. 'God sanctifies persons and not stimulus–response patterns or cultural excretions.'[39] Johnson's concept of moral fault does try to harmonise the teaching of Scripture and the findings of empirical research and, like Jones, offers us a more nuanced account with regard to individual responsibility as the cause of our psychological problems. This approach avoids a naïve and rigid insistence on moral culpability for every 'evil' that befalls us. The Waverley Model has a 'high view' of personal sin as a causal agent of personal problems, but falls short of mere moral determinism by including awareness of how the Fall has weakened our bodies. It does not emphasise systemic powers as a significant causal agent, and to this degree is perhaps an over-individualised model.

Some modern critics of the idea of sin dislike it because they see it as too individualistic. This is often based in Christian tradition, eg the Seven Deadly Sins (all internal to the individual). Starkey comments on this:

By now it will also be clear that this is inadequate as a balanced description of the biblical pictures of sin. These include the idea that sin is a whole matrix or environment in which we are embedded. Sin can be corporate as well as individual, affecting families, neighbourhoods, companies and nations. Once again, the critics offer a helpful corrective to an unbalanced, uncritical picture of sin as a single person doing something wrong. As we have found, the biblical doctrine proves to be broader, more incisive and more up to date than its critics.[40]

Biddle insightfully offers a more socially dynamic account for what Johnson has defined as 'moral fault'. It emphasises the limits of our freedom and culpability for destructive outcomes by emphasising the powerful reality of systemic pressures.

Starkey's categorisation of five main biblical images of sin points to a multi-dimensional concept. Specifically 'alien power' and 'matrix' are images that extend beyond the individual. Biddle agrees with Starkey, arguing that the Bible regards sin and its consequences as an 'organic continuum' between self and 'other'. He states:

A balanced view of sin notes that sin's impact on the world reverberates throughout the sinner's environment, across space and time. In this sense sin becomes a cause. It creates a distorted environment that is the precondition for the sins of others.[41]

In the light of the above, we avoid a reductionist model of sin – individual or social, internal or external; instead we may conclude that sin's causes are dialectic, dynamic and multifaceted.

Summary and evaluation

The importance of adopting a view of sin that combines both individual and systemic perspectives has been demonstrated – a 'both/and' approach better captures the biblical image of sin rather than an 'either/or' choice. Various scholars who take this position have been cited representing both theological and psychological disciplines: Collins, Jones and Butman, Shields and Bredfelt from the latter; Starkey, Biddle and McFadyen from the former. Whereas Crabb did not include the physical area of functioning, the Waverley Model's inclusion of the latter is particularly helpful in giving scope to articulate the limits of our individual culpability for the problems we face. However, this needs to be extended to include the impact of our external contexts (developmental and contemporary) in order to account for the fuller biblical picture. One practical outworking of this last point is that the Waverley Model's diagram requires modification in order to make clearer the impact that systemic powers have on our core spiritual self. This would then broaden Johnson's helpful notion of 'moral fault'. In Pauline theology, weakness (the issue at stake for Johnson) is embodied in the flesh (Rom. 5:6–8) and is thus an important category for understanding people both pre- and post-conversion. For Paul, weakness ultimately shows itself in death, but interestingly for our discussion, this outworking is not just a consequence of personal sin alone, but is also derived from our identification 'systemically' with Adam in his fall and the subsequent powers that reign over us. This view of sin, historical, systemic and personal, gives weight to the notion of depravity, ie it is our fleshly starting point and thus must be taken seriously when offering explanations of pathology. Schreiner states the case clearly:

> *Human beings do not enter the world in a neutral state or slightly inclined to evil, according to Paul. They are polluted by the sin of Adam and enter the world as sinners, condemned and destined for death... Christ is the head of the new humanity and Adam is the head of the old.*[42]

In this respect, it is important that the Waverley Model's emphasis on personal sin as a significant causal agent of pathology should not be lost. Indeed it should be emphasised albeit in a context beyond the individual. This provides a counter-balance to any possible moral reductionism.

Image of God

Within the order of the canon we are first introduced to the concept of being 'made in God's image' amidst the story of creation in the opening chapter of Genesis: 'Let us make mankind in our image, in our likeness... So God created mankind in his own image, in the image of God he created them; male and female he created them' (Gen. 1:26–27).

This is a profound truth within the Christian faith, the meaning of which has been much debated down through the centuries. A variety of interpretations have been developed, as Scripture itself does not conclusively work out the theological meaning. Grudem gives a general interpretation of 'image' and 'likeness' – we are made like God and made to represent Him. This view, he believes, is how the original hearers of Genesis would have understood the phrases. However, he is dubious as to whether we can exceed this general statement with confidence. Hoekema believes that there is no essential difference between 'image' and 'likeness'. Likewise, Calvin did not perceive any significant difference in the meaning, believing that 'likeness' was added as an exposition of 'image'. Smail, whilst acknowledging that in many ways we are different from God, agrees that likeness explains the meaning of image as a real resemblance to God. Ferguson backs up Smail's point in asserting that 'likeness' qualifies 'image' in two ways: negatively, in that our resemblance is limited; positively, in that we should live like him as a 'created analogy'.

In the early centuries of Christianity both Irenaeus and Tertullian distinguished between 'likeness', which was seen as our spirituality, (believed to have been lost by the Fall) and 'image', which was interpreted as our humanity (not lost at the Fall). Defining the 'image', the Waverley Model Trainers' Notes state: 'To be made in God's image means that we have within us the capacities of personhood, enabling us both to relate to God, and represent Him on the earth.'[43] Not all theologians would universally accept this statement and its emphasis. Historically four views have been prevalent, and in the light of Grudem's comment regarding difficulty in pinning down the precise meaning of 'image', and from the vantage point of post-modernity, I will outline a view that attempts to harmonise the traditional divides. This approach will draw together the internal capacities and relational elements within the Waverley quotation above to form one working model.

Image as structural (substantive)

'Image' has often been viewed as referring to the qualities or capacities that humans possess which make them distinct from the rest of the created order and because these correlate with qualities found in God, they make us like Him. Grenz further asserts that this view is, 'perhaps the best known and historically the most widely held understanding of the imago Dei'.[44] As already observed, Irenaeus saw the image and likeness as referring to humanity's spiritual and rational capacities; Aquinas takes a similar view. Augustine's view focused on the image as our capacities of memory, will and intelligence – 'the footsteps of the Trinity'.[45] Calvin considered the image in broader terms, stating, 'the proper seat of the image is in the soul'.[46] By this Calvin meant every facet of our humanity that surpasses that of animals. Calvin includes the body within his idea of image on the grounds that:

> *the corporeal dimension of human life bears witness in some way*
> *to the image of God… the teaching that God created humans in*
> *the image of God is essential for the incarnation, for it provides an*
> *ontological basis for God's Son clothing himself in human flesh.[47]*

The issue of physicality has implications for counselling – where the relational style of the counsellor, as a physical presence, has (as research shows) seen to be a crucial variable in determining client change.

More recently, a popular approach within the structural (substantive) tradition defines 'image' on the basis of communicable attributes, ie those elements of personality we share with God. This is contrasted with other elements of God's personality that we do not share, eg He is everywhere; we are not. Berkhof illustrates this approach well; indeed his table of contents reveals how he works out the above method. Of particular note are communicable attributes, which are outlined as: spiritual, intellectual, moral and taking dominion. Berkhof favours the above approach, believing it brings into focus the similarities and differences between God and humanity. He also qualifies the overarching labels used:

> *Remember that none of the attributes of God are incommunicable in the sense that there is no trace of them in man, and that none of them are communicable in the sense that they are found in man as they are found in God.[48]*

Their metaphoric nature is similar when used with inanimate and animal imagery, for example God as a 'rock' or a 'lion'. However, this is not always so when perfections are used, for example, love and wisdom. Such analogies may literally be true to God. Indeed, Hebblethwaite justifies this use of language on the basis of the incarnation. Despite awareness of God's transcendence and 'otherness', in defence of the use of human analogies Hebblethwaite states:

> *There nevertheless exists a resemblance between God and man, made in his image, which legitimates these personal analogies that are not, as metaphors are, inextricably bound up with imperfection.[49]*

Rae makes similar points in noting the historically cautious position regarding the use of God-human analogies. He includes Hellenistic philosophers (Heraclitus and Xenophanes); Aramaic translations of the Old Testament (all avoid use of such analogies); the Septuagint; Patristics (like Clement of Alexandria, Gregory of Nazianzus and John of Damascus) and Calvin; all took a similar stance. Harrison, on the other hand, in light of humanity's fallen state emphasises an essential difference between God (persons in unison) and humankind (persons in isolation). As a result, she asserts that comparisons between the divine and human must be avoided. Some have attempted to avoid such analogies by making statements relating to humanity as a whole as opposed to founding similarity upon a single attribute. However, Torrance reasons that at whatever level a divine-human comparison is made, the same criticism could apply. Rae balances the caution regarding God-human analogies, which at worst can lead to idolatry (making God in our image), with an emphasis on God's revelation ultimately in Christ – God is no longer like a human, but is a human. This Christ-centred horizon (as opposed to Harrison's horizon of human 'fallenness') gives more emphasis to the propriety of careful use of human analogies. Lastly, Berkhof points out the term 'person' is not used of God in the Old and New Testaments, but the Hebrew word, *panim* and the Greek *prosopon* are closely related to this idea. However, Berkhof does state that where God's presence is personal in both testaments, the use of human analogies will only make sense if: 'the being to whom they apply is a real person with real attributes even though it be without human limitations'.[50] In this light, Berkhof's point helps guard us against literalism (God did not literally stretch out the heavens as a curtain), but he did really initiate and do something as a choosing being. This position thus avoids the other extreme of making the analogies redundant.

Image as functional (dominion)

Here the imago Dei refers not to our essential 'make up', ie faculties that we possess, but to the way humans exercise dominion over creation. This view utilises an interpretive approach where the meaning of image is derived from the immediate co-text (literary context) of Genesis 1:26 and the other relevant passages, eg humanity as God's image in the 'new creation' context of Genesis 9:1–3; Psalm 8; and Hebrews 2:5–9, where Christ the 'New Man' awaits the fullness of dominion and is the image of God. Berkouwer states that, 'the image of God consists in man's dominion, his lordship over the other creatures'.[51] Smail points out that the mandate to have dominion in Genesis provides the theological basis for the use of science, which has 'exposed and actualised the hidden potential of the created world'.[52] This application has relevance for the issue of integrating theology and psychology. Integration such as this need not be anti-biblical, nor be used in a manner which undermines biblical authority or personal faith because it is conceived as a direct outworking of God's commission in Genesis.

Whilst this view can be understood as trying to make sense of relevant scriptural texts, the specific conclusion drawn from the texts, as outlined above, is questioned. Ferguson argues that dominion is a function of the image, not its definition, ie dominion is a consequence, a subsequent outcome, not the essence of what is meant by being made in God's image. Similarly, Erickson considers dominion to be outworking of image rather than an explanation of what it means. Bird takes the opposite view, that the two declarations in Genesis 1:26, namely that humankind is made in God's image and has dominion over creation, belong to a 'single thought complex'. Additionally, Bird argues that within the creation narrative as a whole, design is linked to function and purpose and as such dominion explains the status and role of Adam amidst creation. Whilst there may not be agreement among scholars as to precisely how the Genesis 1:26–28 passage is exegeted regarding dominion, a sole focus on this may be regarded as selective – in Genesis 1:28 there is also the command to 'be fruitful and multiply'. Consideration of this matter proves difficult when applying it to Christ, who is 'the image' (Col. 1:15) and 'the exact representation of his being' (Heb. 1:3). The previous verse (27) links fruitfulness with male and female sexuality in marriage. As Christ did not marry or physically procreate, He would, on this rendering, not fully image God.

Image as relational

Erickson notes that the functional interpretation of imago Dei draws on the philosophy of functionalism or pragmatism, which was popular in the twentieth century. Likewise, Shults shows how the relational view of imago Dei has become prominent as existential philosophy has become influential. Erickson explains the impact of existentialism on imago Dei as underpinning the relational view that de-emphasises essence or substance. He argues that modernism asks the analytical questions, 'What is it?' and 'How does it work?' whereas existentialism asks, 'Is it?' and 'Does it exist?' Reality rather than being in need of analysis and dissection needs to be created, encountered and experienced. Thus for Barth, we image God as we mirror the relationships between the divine Persons of the triune God:

> *We are bold to make the comparison that, as the three Trinitarian*
> *modes of the divine being do not limit and complete each other*
> *as part of the Godhead but are one God in a three-fold identity,*
> *so each of the modes includes the other two within itself and is*
> *within the other.*[53]

Such a conception of human personhood begins to break down the absolute distinctions between persons, as in structural models which emphasise 'self in isolation'. Other-centeredness becomes a primary facet in what it means to image God. In the same way, Jesus' identity is wrapped up in being the Son of the Father.

Grenz summarises the preceding point well when he states, 'The relational understanding of the imago Dei moves the focus from noun to verb.'[54] Grenz cites Hefner and Ramsey as arguing the case that Augustine was 'sensitive' to a relational view of imago Dei, albeit within a predominantly structural view. More explicitly, Brunner advocates the value of existentialist philosophy with regard to its impact on biblical theology. He credits Kierkegaard, Buber and Ebner as examples of such influential thinkers, the legacy of which led theologians to 'abandon the historical form of the doctrine'.[55] 'The image is not something of the past, but confirms us as the core and ground of our own existence.'[56]

Barth, on the other hand, regards image as nothing to do with what a human is or does, but as something which arises out of God's desire for humankind to be His partner. As a result, both God and humans experience 'I–Thou' confrontation. Grenz aligns himself with imago Dei as referring to our other-centeredness, where 'self-fulfilment' is understood in relation to others. He believes this emphasis is due to the demise of modernity and its focus on self as self-centred essence. Grenz gives Barth the credit for a renewal of interest over the past one hundred years regarding views of the Trinity in terms of a social analogy, and that this, in turn, has impacted theological anthropological formulations. Recent relational perspectives have, in turn, expanded the notion of relating to another person or persons in order to image other-centeredness, and focus on a relational context that includes the environment and the cosmos.

Middleton exemplifies this well: the image in Genesis 1 functions as a critique of Mesopotamian ideologies in two distinct issues: firstly, in answering the question, 'Who are we?', the response relates to all humanity alike, imaging God – not merely an elite – for example, kings representing God on earth.

Secondly, in answering the question, 'Where are we?' a clearly good creation is outlined where God is in harmony with what He has created, both human and non-human. Middleton goes on to emphasise the importance of linking the two levels of question:

> *The full-fledged ideology critique of Genesis 1 in other words,*
> *consists not simply in an exalted vision of human identity and*
> *agency, but one grounded in a larger vision of the world as God's*
> *good creation. Together, this two-pronged ideology critique calls*
> *for all humanity (including Israel) to exercise power differently*
> *from anything implied by cosmogenic conflict.*[57]

Such a broad interpretation of relational imaging has implications for human wellbeing which requires an ecological dimension, an attention not only to persons in community, but also their relationship with the wider environment which might include, for example, the impact of housing and working conditions.

Fretheim also encourages us to understand the Fall and its restoration as universal, arguing for a process leading to originating sin in the sense of it becoming all-pervasive. If both Fretheim and Middleton are correct in their understandings then there are significant implications for how we make sense of what it means to restore the image, which is a central facet of Hughes' counselling model. The key Genesis passages may need to extend beyond fellow human beings to a wider environmental and cosmic perspective. Full restoration and its ongoing implications for healthy human functioning will likely be understood in broader terms than an individual turn to Christ in faith, the impact of a fallen environment will still be experienced. As such our counselling models could account for this ongoing level of problem and its effects on the human personality; Seasonal Affective Disorder (SAD) may be just one example of this effect. The amended Waverley Model proposed in this book better portrays this level of interaction than does Hughes' traditional diagram, (see Appendices A and B).

In another model, McFadyen articulates a theory of human personhood in terms of being constituted by relationships, both divine and human. His model is derived from an analogy with God as Trinity – if the Trinitarian Persons exist 'in and for the others', then our personhood likewise is to be defined 'in relation to others'. He thus states:

> *the Father, Son and Spirit are neither simply modes of relations*
> *nor absolutely discrete and independent individuals, but Persons*
> *in relations and only through relations. Persons exist only as they*
> *exist for others, not merely as they exist for themselves.*[58]

Importantly however, McFadyen retains a sense of individual uniqueness, the result of our individual relations to specific people, and also comments: 'If persons are what they are only through their relations with others it must also be the case that their identities are formed through the others and the ways in which the others relate to them.'[59]

McFadyen uses the central metaphor of 'compounded sedimentation' from the history of our interactions with others to explain individual personality differences. Harris, however, critiques McFadyen's emphasis by raising concerns that it leads to an understanding of people as socially determined. Harris, on the other hand, prefers something more consistent and continuous than particular relationships in order to define us as persons, specifically noting that such consistency is required for redemptive transformation to occur. In concluding, Harris draws upon a substantive emphasis in defining human identity. Our relationality is regarded as being founded upon capacities which enable us to do the relating, for example decision making and perception of the existence of another. Functionally, the former relating cannot exist without the latter capacities, but the latter can without the former. Harris illustrates her point by reference to the fact that an animal brought up in the dark retains the capacity to see if subsequently brought into the light.

Perhaps, however, Harris' critique concerning McFadyen's perceived social determinism is unwarranted. Whilst McFadyen rightly emphasises the significance of our social contexts in shaping us as persons, he falls short of determinism, still retaining the belief that we are partly free and autonomous subjects. Indeed, he uses the concept of being 'centred' as a way of explaining both how we reflect upon our experiences in a unique manner and hence respond in a way that may be self-generated, thus retaining the notion of personal responsibility for our actions. As such, McFadyen strikes a welcomed balance by avoiding the unhelpful and invalid extremes of absolute freedom, which ignores the contextual powers that influence and shape our choices, and which on its own leads to a moral reductionism. He also avoids the alternative of social determinism, which leaves no room for an ethic of personal responsibility and is unable to explain how people can and do transcend their own histories.

In principle, Hughes bridges traditional divides when he stresses relationality as essential, yet emphasising a structural account of 'image'. This perspective mirrors McFadyen's dual emphasis: 'Social life and communication are founded on bodiliness, and interpersonal communication is both a social and a bodily activity… anchored firmly in a social world.'[60] Furthermore, Christ as the perfect human brings together the themes of relationality and bodiliness and so an exploration of Christ as the image is necessary.

Christ as the Imago Dei

Whether or not the imago Dei is understood in terms of our constitutional faculties, functioning or relationality, the New Testament views salvation in terms of humanity being 'conformed to the image of his Son' (Rom. 8:29). This purpose in salvation follows from the idea in the New Testament of Jesus as the 'image of God'. Particularly in Pauline theology, Jesus is presented as the 'last Adam' who, in contrast with the 'first Adam', was without sin and so shows us (images) our true humanity as God created us to be. As Grenz notes, whereas the

Old Testament passages relate 'being made in God's image' to all humankind, the New Testament focus relates the idea first to Christ alone, and then by extension to the believing communities. It follows then that God's goal for the Church, and indeed for every Christian, is maturity in Christ (Eph. 4:13) and this equates to being conformed to His image (Rom. 8:28,29; 12:1–2; 2 Cor. 3:18).

If this is so, the goal of Christ-likeness fosters a renewing of 'the image' (a central aim of the Waverley Model) which may be pursued in counselling, especially where a client professes a Christian faith. Holiness is thus seen as a way of life which yields true happiness. Surveying numerous counselling books, Anderson, Zuehlke and Zuehlke, suggest that lists of counselling goals presumed to help counselees include: changing behaviours; attitudes and values; teaching of social, personal and communication skills; encouraging recognition and expression of emotions; and offering support amidst troubled times. However, whilst agreeing that such goals are sometimes relevant for both secular and Christian counselling, they challenge the latter to include, where appropriate, the gospel message and a call for clients to commit their lives to Jesus Christ. This goal is seen as central to those who share the unique purpose of a Christian world-view – to follow Jesus Christ. We are faced with the issue of whether a living faith and wholehearted following of Jesus Christ has any bearing on our healthy functioning.

The presence of some Christlike qualities within the therapist can facilitate health. The divine Son's incarnate identification with us by entering our world provides a paradigm model for counselling, where the counsellor, like Christ, shares in the client's suffering by his or her compassionate presence. Specifically, it is the work of the Holy Spirit that enables people to reflect Christ, 'promoting the quality of life in his people that he himself had lived out'[61] (see 1 Thess. 3:12). This issue is a major one, and will be developed later in Chapter 5, 'Model of Psychotherapy'. The Son's incarnation provides us with a 'concrete' model of other-centred love, which we may imitate for others as he continues to sustain us. God 'comforts us in all our troubles, so that we can comfort those in any trouble with the comfort we ourselves receive from God' (2 Cor. 1:4).

Imago Dei and the Waverley Model

Having made the point earlier that in terms of imago Dei, the Waverley Model falls within a traditional substantive approach, it is also significant to note that, within the Waverley literature Hughes' emphasis upon relationality provides a way of bridging traditional anthropological divides. Russell's critique of Zizioulas' relational approach (which Russell regards as paradigmatic of relational approaches where God as Trinity is articulated in perichoretic terms) centres on his concern that we take care not to lose the individual person amidst our corporate identity. A substantive perspective focuses on the individual but de-emphasises contextual factors. Can we hold both together in order to gain the benefits of both systems? Such an approach can make sense in the light of Goldingay's assertion that being 'made in God's image' is an 'extremely opaque expression, open to our reading into it whatever we wanted to emphasise about humanity's nature'.[62] He advises us to take the phrase 'made in God's image' as a symbol rather than a concept, by which he ironically means a kind of 'image' rather than something definite and precise. Such an understanding is then used to approach the subject of image in a creative open-ended way, rather than attempting to be too dogmatic and prescriptive – a stimulus to thought, as much as a constraint on thought. In view of this, we may seek to bring together possible aspects of truth that the different traditions open up to us which could transcend the boundaries of each perspective alone. McMinn and Campbell's Integrative Psychotherapy model is founded upon such a stance; it brings together relational, structural and functional perspectives as the three domains in which people operate. The alternative is to approach the subject in a polarised manner, forcing a choice between each approach as if one has exclusive insight on truth and logic – a stance that does not carry much weight given the lack of clear evidence. Vitz cites Augustine as doing just this (transcending traditionally held points of demarcation), 'In God there are no accidents, only substance and relation.'[63] Similarly, Vitz offers his own model, 'Substance and relationship are each jointly necessary, but not individually sufficient determinants of personality.'[64] Holding the two historical systems together (substantive and relational) in order to gain their benefits is an approach for which Smail argues:

> *If we think that individuals are ultimate and relationships*
> *subsequent, we will understand ourselves and all that we do in*
> *one way; if we think that it is relationships that shape individuals*
> *we will understand it in another way, and if… we see ourselves*
> *as persons in relationship, we will understand it in a third way,*
> *which, as I will be trying to argue refuses the alternatives of the*
> *other two and does justice to what is of value in each of them.*[65]

Specifically, Smail regards human faculties such as body, soul (here taken as our capacity to feel, think and choose) and spirit not as component parts of a whole person, but as descriptions of the whole self in various sets of relationships. Whilst there have been different ideas regarding how many 'component' parts constitute our humanity, increasingly the unity of the self has been emphasised. N.T. Wright concurs with Milne and Smail's perspectives. He states:

> *Just as, for Paul soma (body) is the whole person seen in terms of*
> *public, space–time presence and sarx (flesh) is the whole person*
> *seen in terms of corruptibility and perhaps rebellion, so psyche*
> *(soul) is the whole person seen in terms of, and from the perspective*
> *of what we loosely call the 'inner life'… Paul can use the word*
> *pneuma (spirit) to refer to the human 'spirit' by which he seems*
> *to mean the very centre of the personality and the point where one*
> *stands on the threshold of encounter with the true God.*[66]

An outline will be undertaken of how the Waverley Model aligns itself with the above approaches, and how attempts to utilise the merits of both relational and substantive models can provide a way forward which necessitates an adaptation of the Waverley Model.

The Waverley Model rightly places great emphasis on the doctrine of the imago Dei. After quoting Genesis 1:26, the Waverley Model Trainers' Notes state, 'Perhaps the greatest single insight a Christian counsellor can have into the nature of human beings is to see that they are bearers of the divine image.'[67] In explaining the meaning of this principle, discussion is centred on the creation narrative and the contrast between communicable and incommunicable attributes, which clearly places Waverley's teaching within the substantive model of imago Dei. This approach to the imago Dei is then explained via discussion of five attributes or 'areas of functioning' – spiritual, rational, volitional, emotional and physical. It is interesting to note that in his later writings, Hughes has substituted the word relational for spiritual, perhaps as a response to the growing emphasis on the latter in contemporary discussions regarding theological anthropology.

Hughes explains God's design in creation as intending to relate first to himself, and then to Eve as the antidote to Adam's aloneness, this being an account that incorporates a symbol of the necessity of human relatedness relevant in principle to all human beings. Concerning the connection between spirit and relationship, Hughes in his book, *The Seven Laws of Spiritual Success*, cites one law as, 'Give yourself to others.' He explains his emphasis as being derived from an understanding of the Trinity as expressed by D. Broughton Knox. Hughes states that what he reads is:

> *The Father loves the Son and gives Him everything. The Son always does that which pleases the Father, the Spirit takes of the things of the Son and always shows them to us. He does not glorify Himself. We learn from the Trinity that relationship is the essence of reality and therefore the essence of our existence, and we also learn that the way this relationship should be expressed is by concern for others. Within the Trinity there is a concern by the persons of the Trinity for one another.*[68]

The central importance of this truth to Hughes cannot be underestimated, especially the statement, 'relationship is the essence of reality'. As the diagram of the original Waverley Model shows (see Appendix A), we see explicitly an individual in isolation, as McFadyen would put it, a 'centred self', a discrete self. Russell points out that the greater the emphasis we place on relationality, the greater will be the necessity to understand the self as open ended, particular, but not a closed entity.

These understandings require a two-fold adaptation of the original

Waverley Model. Firstly, the 'individual person', as a whole functioning entity, must also be envisaged in an open-ended way, not in total isolation. We are not totally discrete, separate or isolated from external contexts and their pervasive influences. Thus it is necessary to add a sixth 'area of functioning' – 'the outside world' (see Appendix B). Thus our 'five areas of functioning' highlighted in the traditional model remain, but are viewed as the faculties which enable us to relate to the 'outside world', a context that is ever present. We are, as Erickson implied, always substance which relates. Benner is therefore helpful when he points out that 'image' when regarded as internal attributes is a useful beginning, but that such approaches miss a more profound attribute which we share with God – our social nature. Secondly, the internal areas of functioning must be incorporated in the Model's diagram as perforated circles, emphasising their dynamic internal-relatedness and inter-connected nature. This undermines any impression that each area is discrete, and operates in isolation.

These considerations also broaden our focus within therapy from learning, to the relational context in which any learning may occur. As mentioned within the brief section 'Christ as imago Dei', God's solution for a fallen world was to send 'One in our likeness' and to share, by His embodiment, our experience of life. This embodied presence of 'Another' who has both compassion and strength, provides a paradigm through which we can explore the importance of relational factors to the therapeutic process.

Summary and Evaluation

In this section four approaches to the issue of imago Dei have been outlined. It has been noted that, whilst in the general historical context the substantive model has dominated theological explanations, over the course of the twentieth century relational models have become prevalent. This shift of emphasis has been linked to changing philosophical persuasions, in particular postmodern critiques of modernity's certitude and fixed sense of reality.

The use of human-centred language has been defended with regard to defining substantive notions of imago Dei via Hebblethwaite's appeal to the incarnation – God as us, not just 'like us' in some metaphoric sense. It has also been demonstrated that an analysis of imago Dei's first occurrence in the Canon (Gen. 1) supports a functional perspective, but that exactly how this is interpreted remains a matter of debate. The relational model with its existential underpinnings has changed the traditional internal focus of 'self-centred' essence to other-centred relationality. Relationality is an important corrective and counterbalance to the internal focus of substantive models; this will reveal itself in the way we construct our ideas regarding personhood (especially to God through Christ). It has been shown that, for Hughes, relationship is an essential element of personhood made in God's image, but that he used this concept in an individualistic, narrow sense, as characterised by a relationship with God through the Christ of our devotions (our inner world) and the Christ of Scripture (the Word of God). A broader Christology which includes 'wisdom' will further develop Hughes' emphasis, so as to account for potential benefits within science and society in general (see Chapter 3, 'Model of Health'). As Pannenberg notes:

> *Every interpretation of Jesus' message has to do justice to the fact that Jesus was concerned for individual persons in their personal relationship to God. Yet his message was not a matter of private devotion. He proclaimed the kingdom of God to come, and with that proclamation he stood in the tradition of the political expectations of the Jewish people. These expectations were concentrated on the hope for a social order of peace and justice.*[69]

Chapter 2

Model of Personality

In this chapter, the Waverley Model's theory of personality will be outlined, firstly by discussing the use of metaphors which compare God and humans. Secondly, a comparison will be made between Hughes' model and that of Crabb, from which it has been developed. Thirdly, links will be made with historical Christian perspectives on human personality; in particular an Augustinian approach will be focused upon, as this provides the clearest counterpart to the Waverley model of personality. The links with both Crabb and Augustine provide contemporary and historical 'comparisons' with which the Waverley Model sits. Lastly, it will be discussed whether the Waverley model of personality is not too complex to be widely accessible, yet at the same time comprehensive so as to address the depth of human nature. These issues will provide a framework against which the strengths and weaknesses of the model can be viewed. In exploring the above issues, the focus will be largely confined to the spiritual area of functioning, because it is the most foundational, distinctive and debatable aspect of Hughes' model.

All models of personality accept that human beings think, feel and act, and that they possess a physical body, although various models may place a different emphasis respectively upon these latter four aspects. Key issues of difference emerge from basic beliefs regarding our core nature, which establishes what motivates the content and direction of thoughts, actions etc.

Anthropomorphic metaphors

Anthropomorphism is the term used to denote portrayals of God in terms of human capacities or attributes (*anthropos* – human; *morphe* – form).

The Waverley model of personality emerges primarily from an understanding of imago Dei in substantive terms. As outlined previously, this is taken as 'five areas of functioning' which we share with God as attributes in common, the exception being the physical area (although in Christ, God did have a body).

> *Although the image of God in man was broken and fragmented, it was not completely lost. Man still functions in the same way he was designed, albeit ineffectively. He is still a spiritual, rational, emotional, volitional and physical being. In other words he is still an Image-Bearer.*[70]

This assertion is backed up with references to anthropomorphic scriptures. Due to the fact that such usage is central to Hughes' theological method, some discussion of this approach is warranted here. The limits of the above method are not articulated by Hughes, whereas Gunton and Caird, amongst others, make the limits explicit. Indeed, Jüngel notes that an anthropomorphic critique precedes biblical writings and is found in context with the earliest known occurrence of the word 'theology'. Having noted that the anthropomorphic metaphors cannot offer an exact comparison, both Gunton and Caird defend their use within theology as a necessary means of making transcendent realities clear via their description within our immediate world. Gunton makes his case partly by showing how science also uses metaphors to grapple with big themes, for instance, the universe described as a machine. His point is that if science, which claims a more precise language, requires 'refuge' in metaphor, how much more will the language of theology when grappling with metaphysical realities, require the use of metaphor. Specifically regarding anthropomorphic usage for descriptions of God, Caird argues that such methods help capture our experiences of a transcendent God, and enable us to 'frame images' which we subsequently use to celebrate and convey these experiences.

In the light of the above point, it is not surprising that for a counselling model developed within an organisation whose mission statement is: 'Applying God's Word to everyday life and relationships', anthropomorphisms play a central role. For Hughes, relationship to God via personal encounter is crucial for healthy functioning (see Chapter 3, 'Model of Health'). As Torrance points out, a loss of anthropomorphic language would jeopardise the importance of and access to intimacy, at least in terms of how such intimacy might, as Caird suggested, be spoken of and hence celebrated publicly or privately. Torrance also articulates 'tensions' around the use of anthropomorphisms in the context of refined theological reflection, ie 'in advancing from the second to the third epistemological level', by which he means from descriptions of God as He is towards us as Father, Son and Holy Spirit (economic) through to who He is in Himself (ontological). Such movement is unlikely for 'lay people' who may not possess such theological sophistication. It could be further argued that a model developed initially for pastoral care contexts requires a focus on aspects of God 'in our realm' (Emmanuel) as opposed to His 'otherness' which might not be experienced as having as much therapeutic immediacy. However, it could be the case that God's transcendence and otherness has a vital function in retaining hope amidst calamity and chaos, ie debilitating experiences will not have the 'last word' as God is 'bigger than them all'.

The above three issues are all grounds for the retention of anthropomorphic language within the context of a biblically-based counselling model. The argument thus stated is pragmatic, rooted in how Scripture might function for an individual. This approach however, need not be regarded as 'less than ultimate (ontological) truth', for as Jüngel asserts, anthropomorphic language needs to be seen as an expression of Scripture's material content – God coming into our world ultimately in Christ in order to help us live differently.

Caird further believes that anthropomorphic language may serve us in attaining God's creation purpose – for humankind to become like God, ie to image Him: 'Man is created to become like God, and the ultimate justification of anthropomorphic language lies in the contribution it makes to the attainment of that goal.'[71] From a more critical stance, Torrance argues against the use of anthropomorphisms in that they assume a general continuity between God and human beings, and in so doing, de-emphasise differences. In general, it is clear that there is no universally accepted theory of interpreting theological language, especially the use of metaphor. McFague puts forward the view that metaphor as a device is largely superfluous and instead ideas could be stated directly. Rae has noted the concern that Scripture itself conveys regarding people's tendency to portray God in human terms. The prohibition of idolatry in Exodus 20:4 makes this clear. Thus the concern not to diminish the otherness of God is at stake. To this end, Heschel points out that such a concern was an anathema for Jewish believers, where the dissociation of God from humankind was a clear presupposition, unlike Greek ideas from where such concerns were imported. Additionally, Heschel alerts us to the difference between anthropomorphic conceptions and anthropomorphic expressions. The use of the latter does not necessarily prove belief in the former. As long as this distinction is held in mind, we can fruitfully embrace this language as a valid descriptive and explanatory category. Heschel explains:

> *Pathos is a thought that bears a resemblance to an aspect of divine reality as related to the world of man. As a theological category it is a genuine insight into God's relatedness to man, rather than a projection of human traits into divinity, as for example in the God images of mythology.*[72]

Whilst we can be clear that metaphors of any type, including anthropomorphisms, are not precise or straightforward descriptions of the objects in view, they are, as Heschel has noted, still 'genuine insights' rather than mere projections invented by humankind. Understood as part of God's gracious accommodation of our finite realms of thought, anthropomorphisms within the Waverley Model must be embraced as 'explanatory tools', albeit not literal ones and so not rejected as 'empty' or 'worthless'.

Hughes' and Crabb's relationality: 'spiritual area' of functioning

Having argued for the validity of anthropomorphic categories within the Waverley Model, the five categories used will now be outlined: spiritual, rational, volitional, emotional and physical. Extensive discussion will be confined to the core spiritual area as this is the model's most distinctive element. This rendering seeks firstly to address contemporary psychological questions regarding the impact of the Fall upon the subjective wellbeing of the first human pair. Additionally, it becomes the means of articulating human suffering in general, rooted in a biblical world-view.

Hughes' specific approach extends a tri-partite model of personhood, and cites 1 Thessalonians 5:23, 'May God himself, the God of peace, sanctify you through and through. May your whole spirit, soul and body be kept blameless at the coming of our Lord Jesus Christ', as paradigmatic. Others would criticise this stance on methodological grounds. Hughes explains further that body, soul and spirit overlap and interrelate. More specifically, body is regarded as the means through which we inhabit the world; spirit as that part of us which relates to God; and soul as being comprised of thoughts, feelings and will, thus making five areas in all. For Hughes, relationships are central facets of our personhood, but of primary importance for personal functioning is our relationship with God which functions via our spiritual area. Hughes depicts the spiritual area in relational terms; derived from his own emphasis, regarding the God revealed in Scripture as a relational God. Crabb's model uses the term 'personal' instead of spiritual (as in Hughes'). However, the meanings each ascribe to these different terms are synonymous. In Crabb's chapter, 'Dependent Beings: People are Personal', he states: 'As image-bearers we long for relationship. As fallen image-bearers we turn away from God to look for it. No wonder God calls us foolish!'[73] So for both Crabb and Hughes, relationship with God is the key issue at the core of our humanity, and for them this mediates our general wellbeing. The Bobgans and Adams, whilst concurring with an emphasis on a God relationship, would be critical of a method which also includes an openness to insights from contemporary psychological theory and technique. Adams further critiques

Crabb's anthropological model on methodological grounds, believing that his model owes more to the influence of contemporary psychologists such as Ellis, Adler and Rogers, than to biblical anthropology. It is evident that Hughes and Crabb are open to the possible benefits of insights from Ellis, Adler, Rogers and others ('Spoiling the Egyptians'). However, Crabb and Hughes' models are not founded upon the work of these psychologists, but are an attempt to make sense of the internal experiences of Adam and Eve pre- and post-Fall. This 'fall' includes awareness of nakedness (Gen. 3:7) and fear (Gen. 3:8): 'The impulse to cover themselves and to hide from God embodies the essential change that has occurred, encompassing shame, self-consciousness, the experience of loss and the awareness of separation from God.'[74] These experiences, as a consequence of the Fall, are taken as protological. There are divergent opinions as to the connection between the account of Genesis chapters two and three and our current experience of suffering. Secondly, Crabb and more explicitly Hughes, utilise modern psychological understanding to fill in detail about which the Bible is not explicit. So Hughes' three core longings of security, self-worth and significance are clearly derived from the work of Erikson (see later in this section). Whilst this method in general is open to criticism from those like Adams and the Bobgans who argue for a 'Bible only' approach, it is consistent with the goals of a systematic theology which, according to Pannenberg, aims at reformulating the eternal truths of Scripture in modern terms that emerge from secular findings. In the contemporary context of Christian counselling, rooted in a biblical world-view, the subjective impact of the Fall upon Adam and Eve becomes a significant point of interest as a potential means of explanation for suffering.

The necessity of relationship (especially to God), is brought into greater focus in Crabb's later writing. In *Connecting:* Healing *for Ourselves and Our Relationships*, he states three core beliefs emerging from his own mid-life crisis:

1. 'The greatest need in modern civilisation is the development of communities – the communities where the heart of God is home'

2. 'We must do something other than to train professional experts to fix damaged psyches… the problem beneath our struggles is a disconnected soul.'

3. 'Beneath what our culture calls psychological disorder is a soul crying out for what only community can provide.'[75]

These statements make clear Crabb's belief that what we may think of as psychological disorders can be reframed as relational problems, and that the ultimate relational healer is God mediated through His church. In light of some neuro-scientific research, it may not be easy to separate 'spiritual area' relational deficits and their impact upon brain development. This adds scientific weight to Johnson's notion of weakness as 'moral fault' (discussed in the last chapter), and promotes the relevance of conceptualising people as dynamic wholes rather than discrete parts. So, whilst Hughes provides a conceptual partition between 'the spiritual' and other 'areas', this appears to emerge from his structural anthropology which is divided functionally, eg the spirit is the 'area' which relates to God. In practice, such demarcation may have a teaching and learning benefit – the complex whole is split into parts for the sake of simplicity. However, the pragmatism rather than the ontology of this position is noted.

Wisdom – a broad relationality

Relational disconnection or connectedness has been a central issue for Crabb from his earliest writings. This emphasis has the broadest explanatory power if coupled with a robust wisdom theology. This helps keep notions of relatedness broad, and so includes both the social world and the natural order. Moltmann states:

> *In revelation theology, it seems that God reveals himself in the events and persons of human history, and is then recognised again in nature. In wisdom theology God is perceived from the life and orders of nature, and then recognised again in human wisdom about life. Instead of God – human being – nature, the order here is God – nature – human being.*[76]

Such a perspective helps make sense biblically of why some people, though not Christian, can lead relatively healthy and productive temporal lives. This avoids an exclusive link between salvation and wellbeing, without discounting the benefits in this respect. Hunter describes wisdom as including the idea of life-long learning that is not especially religious, or a natural possession, but which may be embraced through discipline and attention to those who are more experienced – in the context of Israel, especially learning within the family via parents. Contemporarily the value for our wellbeing of such family wisdom will depend, in part, on its links with God's creation order – there is always the danger that human wisdom is merely 'wise in their own eyes' (Isa. 5:21; 47:10; Job 5:13; 15:8; 37:24; Prov. 3:7; 26:5,12).

Following Crabb's insistence on the relevance of relationship with God to our notions of mental health, he states three basic assumptions, one of which is that Christ offers us unique resources to help resolve every non-organic problem. Hughes agrees with these sentiments in his early writing on counselling matters. In his later writing he offers a summary of his ideas:

> God has designed us as relational beings who are meant first to relate to him and then to others. The closer we relate to him and draw from his resources, the more equipped we are to relate well to others and cope with whatever life brings.[77]

Having shown how important Hughes and Crabb believe the spiritual area to be in shaping us as persons, it is necessary to outline how Hughes develops this idea.

Relationality from the perspective of Genesis

Hughes introduces us to pre-Fall humanity in the context of the opening chapters of Genesis: 'We learn a good deal... by taking an in-depth look at what went on in the lives of the first human pair – Adam and Eve.'[78] In a chapter in which Hughes outlines his ideas regarding God's creation of Adam and Eve, he concludes: 'Without doubt Adam and Eve lived in a perfect world. No sin, no disturbance of spirit, no suffering, no shame. The Almighty declared it 'very good'. But not for long.'[79] In offering a rationale for his model of personality, Hughes does not show awareness of other possible biblical starting points (eg Jesus), and thus does not defend his method as being preferable to others. For Thiselton, using 'the Garden' as a means of understanding the human condition promotes relationality as a core feature, whatever varied emphasis within that theme is adopted. From such a starting point, it becomes hard to include a broader wisdom Christology (especially its social, cultural and scientific elements) as these potential elements of God's grace have not been developed at this point in the unfolding biblical story. Wenham, arguing that the theme of Genesis as a whole is one of redemption, believes chapters one and two describe our original state to which we will return once the consequences of the Fall (see especially Genesis, chapter three to eleven) are overcome, which will occur once all the patriarchal promises are fulfilled. Hughes leaves us in no doubt that he similarly believes that the most important factor that can affect our personality is connection to God. Under a heading 'Spiritual Needs' he states: 'The greatest need of every individual is to have a relationship with God.'[80] There are numerous empirical studies that give weight to the value of religious belief as a critical influence upon the development of healthy personality as it transitions through developmental life stages. It was explained earlier in this chapter that Hughes regards humans as having five areas of functioning with which we may potentially enter into, and experience relationship with others.

The spiritual area is separated into three capacities: security, self-worth and significance. Hughes' three spiritual capacities are not explicitly articulated in the Genesis account, but may be inferred by contrasting the pre- and post-Fall narratives where the initial relationship with God has been interrupted by sin. According to Hughes, the fulfilment of these core (crucial) longings – desires, needs, 'thirsts' – form the foundation of a healthy personality. The Waverley Model Trainers' Notes state: 'Some needs are crucial, if they are not met, then we simply cannot function as human beings.'[81] This is a reference to the human needs for security, self-worth and significance, a principle expanded upon by Hughes. This is so important for his model of personality that I will utilise an extensive quote:

> *There is a longing in the soul, a thirst for relationships that is*
> *powerful, that though hidden, ignored, over-laid, and even denied,*
> *has a powerful pull in our personalities. These longings are there*
> *because we were built to relate first to God and then to others.*
> *When we don't function in this way, then deep down we sense a*
> *high degree of spiritual discomfort because we are not relating to*
> *God and others in the way we were designed. It is impossible for*
> *people to have a clear sense of their identity – who they really are*
> *– outside of a relationship with God: To paraphrase the famous*
> *words of the fourth century preacher Augustine: 'We were made*
> *by God, and made for God, and our identity will never be fully*
> *complete until we relate to God.'[82]*

A New Testament theology of redemption includes within it the relevance
for healthy functioning of restoring the human-God relationship so crucial
for Hughes' model.

In an introduction to the spiritual area of functioning, under the heading
'Biblical and Theoretical Foundations', the Waverley Model Trainers' Notes
pose the question: 'What must it have been like for Adam and Eve in the
Garden of Eden?'[83] In answering the question, primary focus is drawn to the
human's relationship with God and what is described as a crucial difference
between God and Adam and Eve – the latter were dependent beings, and thus
healthy functioning was rooted in their relationship with God. In defining
the three crucial capacities of security, self-worth and significance, security
is taken to mean the experience of belonging and being unconditionally
loved. Self-worth is defined as a person's sense of being valued or viewed as
worthwhile by another. This social dimension again reinforces the relational
aspect of Hughes' model of personality. Significance is defined as a sense of
achievement, a sense of purpose which yields awareness that our lives are
meaningful. To put it succinctly, Hughes states: 'Identity depends on three
things – a sense that one is unconditionally loved, a sense of one's value, and
a sense of meaning and purpose.'[84]

Hughes and social ontext: psychosocial and social learning theory

The three core longings, as inferred by Hughes from the Genesis story, correspond with Erikson's first three stages of psychosocial development, from which Hughes appears to have derived them. Hughes articulates his three foundational longings in unfolding developmental terms. Not all would agree with this stage hierarchy approach. Stern challenges the belief that pathology arises from developmentally sensitive periods. Others have critiqued stage theories like Erikson's on cultural grounds, regarding them as a Western imposition that does not allow for variation of cultural experience. Additionally, it is important to note that if Adam and Eve are to be regarded as prototypes of current human experience, there are, from a straightforward reading of the creation narratives, significant differences between them and ourselves as contemporary people. Firstly, Adam and Eve did not enter life from a context of 'fallenness'; secondly, they were initially devoid of corporate community; and thirdly, they start life as 'fully functioning adults', and so do not develop through childhood as we are compelled to do. These differences alert us to the dangers of inferring too many correlations from the 'Garden' context to our contemporary experience, beyond the most general and profound. In this light, the attempt of Hughes and Crabb to illuminate issues relating to our core sense of self (spiritual nature) pre- and post-Fall are reasonable and laudable; for as Brunner states:

> *The most powerful of all spiritual forces is man's view of himself,*
> *the way in which he understands his nature and his destiny;*
> *indeed it is the one force which determines all the others which*
> *influence human life.*[85]

Contemporarily, therefore, a person's view of themselves will in part emerge from the specific localised and variable conditions into which they were born. By grasping this issue of profound difference when compared to Adam and Eve's origins, a framework through which we may understand individual difference of personality is provided. Regarding contemporary development,

Hughes believes that the need to belong dominates the first few months of life, and that if this goal is not achieved, deep anxiety and an inability to trust develop. This lack of trust (Erikson's stage one, trust versus mistrust in the first year of life) denies us the internal sense of security we were designed to experience. The second need, to find an adequate self-worth, corresponds to Erikson's stage two (autonomy versus shame and doubt, years one to two). Hughes states, 'As we grow a little older, beyond the first year of life, a second basic need becomes prominent – the need for self-worth.'[86] Hughes defines self-worth as a composite sense of our value as a person, which is derived from the internalised messages of 'significant others': 'Seeing how worthwhile we are in someone else's eyes contributes greatly to our own sense of worth.'[87] In particular, Hughes gives prominence to parental messages of worth. However, Hughes does not view people as passive recipients of these messages, but rather as active interpreters. Hence people co-create these messages; this leads to individuals interpreting the same messages differently, and gives rise to potential disparity between any specific message given and that which is believed to be true. Hughes articulates this dynamic as follows: 'I am not what I think I am; I am not what you think I am; I am what I think you think I am.'[88] In Erikson's terminology, the need for a self with which we may be satisfied is opposed by fears of shame and resultant self-doubts, which arise from the perceived demands of others that the self (body and thoughts) be viewed as evil and dirty. This emphasis aligns Hughes within social learning theory where shaping factors are reciprocated between the social environment and an individual's construction of it.

Given the importance of social learning theory to Hughes' notions of developmental factors, a brief outline of the theory will be helpful in order to grasp its essential premises and the context from which it developed. Albert Bandura developed social learning theory, extending Miller and Dollard's Social Learning and Imitation Model. Essentially, they were behaviourists who believed our environment determined our behaviour. Rotter also influenced Bandura, believing that both internal psychological and external environmental factors influence our development. Bandura adopted a behavioural learning theory stance in the 1970s: 'From the social learning perspective, human nature is characterised as a vast potentiality that can be fashioned by social influences into a variety of forms.'[89] However, by 1986, Bandura had incorporated a more cognitive element:

> *From the social cognitive perspective human nature is characterised by a vast potentiality that can be fashioned by direct and observational experience into a variety of forms within biological limits.*[90]

Bandura has appeared to have been influenced by the cognitive re-evaluation of the 1960s that emphasised an individual's information-processing activity, which is believed to mediate events and behaviours. Key to Bandura's theory is the reciprocal nature of self construction and social environment, which presents a space for individual responsibility amidst powerful social forces. Martin and Hill conclude as follows:

> *Like Scripture, Social Learning theory sees a person as an active rational agent, responsible for actions and able to change behaviours, yet ever subject to the influences of the social environment.*[91]

This approach is believed to have gained a wide acceptance amongst psychologists, partly because of its broad conception of shaping factors. Biblically, therefore, a laudable balance is struck between persons as active responsible agents who can change behaviour, and those who are also continually subject to powerful social and spiritual forces (see section on 'Sin' in Chapter 1). Ironically, social learning theory has been criticised for not sufficiently emphasising social influences beyond modelling and reinforcement. Interestingly, in light of a theology where Adam and Eve are regarded as prototypes of humanity in general, Piaget's ideas about general structural reorganisation rooted in developmental experiences are excluded. According to the creation account, unlike us, Adam and Eve start their human existence as fully formed adults. Hearnshaw articulates well the interrelated environments that Hughes acknowledges impact upon us –

internal, external and historical. In order to capture these complexities it is necessary to utilise an extensive quote. Hearnshaw states:

> *Action implies an agent... it is generally... intentional; it is commonly goal-directed, and more often than not structured according to conventions and rules... The majority of human actions take place in a social context, and this social context is an integral part of any action. Action cannot be understood apart from the time dimension, and this means, on the one hand, the consideration of history both of the social group and the individual, and, on the other, the expected future towards which the action is directed.[92]*

Of the three dimensions – internal, external and historical, Hughes' focus is most explicitly on the internal (five areas of functioning), although this is placed in historical context (see phase one of the Waverley three-phase counselling process). The impact of social context is not a significant focus in Hughes' model. This book is, in part, an attempt to rectify the relative absence by conceiving of personhood in a more open-ended manner. Consequently it can provide a basis for explaining how recent research increasingly gives weight to this dimension, and hence the significant impact relationality has in explaining both pathology and health. This will be explored in the later chapters on 'Model of Health'; 'Model of Abnormality' and 'Model of Psychotherapy'.

Compared with Crabb's model, Hughes adds self-worth as an additional core category. The distinction between security (unconditional love) and self-worth (value) may not be obvious, as it could be argued that to experience unconditional love from another implies our value, particularly in view of Hughes' definition of 'worth' which is not based on what we do, but on who we are. Hughes acknowledges the difficulty of a clear distinction, but argues that security yields a sense of being 'cherished', whilst self-worth yields a sense of being 'worthwhile'. Beyond use of these two adjectives, Hughes offers no further explanation in support of his distinction. As Hughes' model was developed from Crabb's, the necessity to justify the additional category rests with Hughes. Hughes' argument is insufficient to support his assertion as his case rests on the use of words which he does not justify linguistically or biblically. To be loved unconditionally for who we are rather than for what we do (the meeting of conditions) must imply intrinsic value which is thus non-dependent. In this case, self-worth is derived from a sense of security (without precluding other possibilities, eg significance). In Crabb's model, our core identity is constituted by our security and significance. If these two elements are core, and are being satisfied, it need not be too extreme an inference to suppose a consequent positive general sense of self, ie a robust self-worth.

The distinctions between Hughes and Crabb need not represent an unbridgeable conceptual chasm, as they may represent a linguistic divide rather than an essential discrepancy. Any difference should also be viewed within the context of what is shared – the centrality of longings and God's ability alone to sufficiently meet them. Additionally, from a contemporary postmodern perspective the emphasis of modernity for 'mathematical' analytic precision may not be sought, and thus differences are made more tolerable and even celebrated. Gunton raises this issue from the context of metaphysical models, where a certain 'openness' and acceptance of the 'finiteness' of any asserted idea is presumed. Gunton equates modernity with an 'excessive veneration of unity'.[93] Likewise, Crabb appears to support Gunton's perspective:

> *No final or closed model of counselling will ever be developed by fallen finite man. The best model will always have ragged edges which can be partially smoothed out only through openness to new thinking and data.*[94]

This book is an attempt to incorporate such 'new thinking and data' into the Waverley Model. Jacobs also warns us against using knowledge too precisely, which can become a battle of 'labelling'. The critiques of Gunton, Crabb and Jacobs apply in the issue of the difference between Crabb and Hughes' particular designations of spiritual needs; any theory of human motivation (Christian or secular, spiritual or psychological) will be caught up with metaphysical and/or transcendent realities, neither of which can be tied down precisely.

Hughes' third core longing is that of significance. In his early writing, the concept is denoted by the verb 'to achieve'. Hughes felt that the cause of adults experiencing constant fear of failure has its genesis in childhood, namely failure to attain valued goals via achievements. Developmentally, Hughes regards the genesis of this 'drive' as arising between the ages of three to five which is illustrative of Hughes' stage related developmental presuppositions. This correlates with Erikson's stage three (initiative versus guilt). Erikson explains that beyond stage two (autonomy), where self-will may be in defiance as an assertion of independence against 'the other', initiative in stage three is more proactive, 'attacking' the world 'out there' so as to be 'on the move' towards something. By significance, Hughes means the desire for a sense of meaning and purpose, which derives from our being made in God's image. This can only be fully realised in relationship with him, thus affirming dependency on God as a core issue. Hughes uses Jeremiah 29:11, "'For I know the plans I have for you," declares the Lord, "plans to prosper you and not to harm you, plans to give you a hope and a future"', as Scriptural support for his assertion as well as citing psychiatrist Victor Frankl. Leaving aside theological debate regarding the generalised application of the prophet's words, the issue of purpose (significance) is helpful at least in exposing the core place of hope in both Hughes' and Erikson's ideas. Erikson states:

> *There is for every child at every stage a new miracle of vigorous unfolding, which constitutes a new hope and a new responsibility for all. Such is the sense and the pervading quality of initiative.*[95]

For Hughes, ultimate hope relating to eternal purpose and significance is a gift from God, hence Hughes' use of Jeremiah 29:11 where God declared His intention to prosper His people and to give hope and a future.

From the context of creation and in particular, the Garden of Eden, Hughes builds his model via an inference of how a close relationship with God would have been experienced. His conclusion was that Adam and Eve would have experienced a high degree of security, self-worth and significance, ie their core identity was fulfilled. He continues that sin severed their relationship with God and consequently the created capacity for security became experienced as insecurity; self-worth as inferiority; and significance as insignificance. He concludes, 'Thus took place the world's first identity crisis.'[96] Hughes thus equates our spiritual area of functioning with our core identity. Hughes' 'crisis' makes sense when viewing imago Dei as relational like McFadyen, where identity is constituted through our responses to the way others relate to us. So whilst Hughes' longings are experienced at the 'core' of personality, they are derived from social relatedness. As McFadyen might define this process, 'our communicative form' (our personalities) emerges from the habitual responses to 'the call' of others, being mistrustful or confident etc.

Crabb's method for establishing a model of personhood is the same as Hughes'. It is founded upon an understanding of what it means to be 'made in God's image', which in turn is worked out according to a long-standing tradition within Christian theology of regarding image in terms of structural capacities or potentials (see 'Image as Structural' Chapter 1). Crabb states: 'We are persons. God is a person. We are like Him in that we possess the elements which together make up personality.'[97] In order to identify which elements constitute 'the image', Crabb advocates listing God's attributes and discerning which ones were communicated to us:

> *We need to ask whether the qualities we identify are*
> *communicable and whether they have in fact been communicated*
> *to us. When we can list the distinctions of personality that both*
> *God and human beings share, then we will have a basic definition*
> *of the image of God.*[98]

In accomplishing this task, Crabb rightly points out that such a method involves making inferences from Scripture in the way it presents God as a person. Like the method adopted by Hughes, it is therefore necessary to give priority to anthropomorphic imagery, the propriety for which has already been argued. At various places in their writings, Crabb and Hughes have used the terms 'spiritual', 'relational' and 'personal' to describe our core capacity as persons. Crabb specifically uses the term 'personal', and in both God and humans he sees a deep longing for relationship (eg Hos. 11:8 and Psa. 42:1; 63:1). Crabb concludes on this issue: 'Both God and man have the capacity to long deeply.'[99] Crabb's language indicates that, for him, communicable capacities define 'image of God' and that these attributes are regarded as analogous not identical.

An individual's volitional response to their constitutional longings is at the centre of Hughes' and Crabb's models. This helpfully guards against a deterministic approach to human functioning, and in so doing promotes particularity and an emphasis on moral responsibility as to how we each try and meet our deep needs.

Human motivation – a biblical theology?

Hughes' and Crabb's understanding of human longings emerge from two biblical concepts: 'innermost being' and 'our soul's deepest thirst', both of which are found, among other places in Scripture, in John 7:37–38. Given the importance of these concepts to both models, the passage will be quoted in full:

> On the last and greatest day of the festival, Jesus stood and said
> in a loud voice, 'Let anyone who is thirsty come to me and drink.
> Whoever believes in me, as Scripture has said, rivers of living
> water will flow from within them.'

There is some dispute on linguistic grounds as to precisely what Jesus is saying about the water symbolism. In the New American Standard Bible translation, from which Crabb quotes, the term 'innermost being' is used instead of 'within' (NIV). The King James rendering is more literal: 'belly'. The Greek word is koilia whose basic and general meaning is a cavity or hollow. In the New Testament, koilia is used to refer literally to the stomach (Matt. 12:40; Rev. 10:9–10); the womb (Luke 1:41–2; 2:21; 11:21; Acts 3:2); and uniquely according to Verbrugge, to the inner person (John 7:38). Adams gives great anthropological weight to the 'inner person', which he believes is best summed up biblically by the word 'heart'. He understands its major thrust throughout Scripture as denoting: 'the entire inner life... the most far-reaching and most dynamic concept of the non-material (or spiritual side of) man'.[100] Crabb concurs with Verbrugge in saying that koilia means literally a stomach, or metaphorically (as in John 7:38) a void, which everyone possesses at the core of their being, which longs to be filled. Beasley-Murray regards the koilia teaching of Christ as applying beyond Christ's immediate audience, having relevance to God's past and future saving acts. In this light there is a warrant for using koilia as a paradigm image. Lincoln clearly makes broad links of a similar kind. Drawing all these connections together, he summarises John's citation as implying that 'Jesus is now the rock from whose words come the waters of new life, the waters of the Spirit, the agent of new birth'[101] (cf. John 3:5–6,8; also John 1:12–13). The imagery of John 7:38 used by Jesus is found in various Old Testament passages and depicts human need and God's provision for it in similar ways. Crabb and Hughes cite a number of such passages as clear evidence that people may be characterised as needy, dependent beings, requiring something essential, ie living water, which they do not intrinsically possess, and which only God can provide in a sustained and sufficient manner. Commenting on similar Old and New Testament passages, Schnackenburg and Brown convey the vital importance of water imagery within a biblical world-view. Citing Grelot, Schnackenburg regards the water imagery at Tabernacles as connecting to both 'end times' life and that of Israel's past desert wanderings, where the rock gushed forth with life-saving water. Schnackenburg concludes:

> *In thinking of this kind, the image of the drawing and outpouring of the water would awaken many associations and call various texts to mind, all within the perspective of the hope of salvation. We may, then, explain the condensed 'saying of Scripture' in John 7:38 as a construction of the evangelist intended to express, in one sentence, all these typological ideas.*[102]

Hughes' and Crabb's central usage of this passage clearly has scholarly support in denoting a profound human state. Brown outlines how the Hebrew word *nefes* (translated either soul or spirit) was seen as the centre of thirst: it originally seemed to mean 'throat'. With this background, we can make a case from Scripture for regarding humanity as needy, with specific longings which are portrayed in embodied form – the throat is thirsty, the belly needs filling.

The two central concepts from which Hughes and Crabb build their models – inner being, and our soul's thirst – converge in John 7:38.

Both Crabb and Hughes use the above concepts as central ideas for understanding human motivation. This core motivation is clearly articulated in relational terms, with primary importance given to our relationship with God. Relational longings (thirsts) are essential aspects of human nature are found throughout Scripture in, for example the prophets Isaiah, Jeremiah and Ezekiel; the psalms; the Gospels; and lastly within the canon in the book of Revelation. This last usage represents a call from God to anyone and everyone to come and drink. Its appeal rests on an individual's awareness of their thirst (longings). Whilst too much could be read into the position of a text, it is not mere coincidence that the last invitation of God to humankind within the canon of Scripture embraces imagery of thirst and water. If Aune is correct, this invitation echoes that of Revelation 21:6b, whose context is eternal, ie in view of everything (God the Alpha and Omega, the Beginning and the End). Given the imprecise nature of metaphor, Thiselton notes that it is always possible to overplay any image. However, in the light of Aune and that cited above, there is reasonable ground not to marginalise this imagery and the truth to which it pertains regarding core issues, literally at the 'heart' of anthropology.

The next two sections will outline a brief history of a theological tradition emphasising inwardness. Starting with Augustine, and re-emerging during the Reformation, it forms a lineage of which the Waverley Model is a part. Baxter and Scougal's theological anthropologies will also be briefly sketched as they represent figures that have had significant influence upon the pastoral thinking and practice of later churches. Whilst the previous section regarding koilia has been functioning as a means of validating the term's significance as a biblical concept of motivation, the texts themselves do not articulate what constitutes 'thirst'. Therefore they cannot be used to verify the Waverley Model's assertion that 'thirst' comprises longings for security, self-worth and significance. This argument has been made already, upon different grounds (see previous section 'Hughes' and Crabb's Relationality').

Augustine and motivation

As will be shown, Augustinian theology provides an historical and theological point of contact for Hughes' model of motivation, and so offers a frame of reference against which strengths and weaknesses may be articulated. As Hurding has summarised, Hughes' model may be depicted as 'a layer theory', comprising five internal areas of functioning with the 'core' being the spiritual area. This focus on internality or inwardness was shared by Augustine who, like Hughes, also emphasised the importance of the 'vertical' relationship with God in shaping personality, and in doing so, de-emphasised the importance of social relationships. This emphasis has been criticised by Gunton who characterises Augustine's approach as leading to individualism and intellectualism at the expense of persons in relationships. This criticism is a moot point for Hughes and Crabb, for as already outlined, relationality is at the heart of their models – security and self-worth in particular, have been articulated, at least in part, as products (McFadyen's 'sediments') of relational experiences. Crabb specifically highlights the importance of the Church community as a place of healing and spiritual growth. These clearly relational ideas however may be undermined by the traditional Waverley Model's diagram which is ostensibly self-contained, apparently unaffected by social conditions, and exclusively internally derived, (see Appendix A). This in turn may be partly derived from the focus given to the pre-Fall Genesis account when building the core of the model. From this context, apart from the two humans, there is no wider community of fellow humans from which to gain support or to find encouragement – they lived in isolation with God. This explains the need to expand the model to include a social dimension, a need facilitated by an amendment to a more open-ended diagram of personality.

Speaking of *Confessions*, probably Augustine's best known work, Brown characterises it as 'a manifesto for the unexpected, hidden qualities of the inner world'.[103] Bailie makes clear his view regarding Augustine's connection with the concept of inwardness: 'Not only, however, does Augustine represent the Cartesian revolution in embryo, but, more importantly, he is the source of the very notion of the 'inner self'.[104] To portray Augustine as founder of the notion of the 'inner self' seems, in the light of Scripture, (Mark 15:1–19; Psa. 51:6; Prov. 20:27; Luke 1:51) to be hyperbolic; however, his stature within early Christianity has undoubtedly led to this notion's adoption down through the centuries. It would therefore not seem to be an exaggeration when Bailie states that: 'Augustine did more to encourage authentic Christian interiority than anyone in the early Church.'[105]

Like Hughes, Augustine's rationale for emphasising the necessity of a relationship with God rests on his assumption regarding human motivation. This centred on a desire to find happiness which ultimately would be satisfied only by God; the parallel with Hughes' model is evident: 'This is happiness to be joyful in Thee and for Thee and because of Thee, this and no other. Those who think happiness is any other, pursue a joy that is apart from Thee and is no true joy.'[106]

As Johnson points out, Augustine's emphasis on motivation rooted in fulfilment of desire was commonplace in his day. However, Augustine's focus on happiness as the possession and enjoyment of God stood in contrast to the Epicureans (happiness in earthly pleasures) as well as the Platonists and Stoics (happiness in rational contemplation of truth).

Desire shapes our view of the dynamics of inwardness, and by doing this links two key issues central to Hughes' and Crabb's models, namely human 'thirst' at the 'core' of our being. Roberts captures this biblical notion as he contrasts 'outer' and 'inner' functioning: 'In this inward dimension, which the Bible calls the 'heart' or 'mind' are found our wishes, cares, intentions, plans, motives, emotions, thoughts, attitudes, and imaginings.'[107]

Whilst Roberts' list extends beyond what may be subsumed under the term 'desire', it is notable that 'wishes', 'intentions', 'plans', and 'motives', do fit within the semantic range of meaning. Hughes and Crabb use the term 'longings' to denote desires; Hughes specifically articulates crucial longings as those belonging to our 'core' spiritual self, and so elevates spirituality as a primary issue. Augustine uses 'longings' to describe this ultimate yearning which he typifies as essential humanity: 'Do we not all long for the future Jerusalem? I cannot refrain from this longing, I would be inhuman if I could.'[108] Making the same point, Vanhoozer cites Augustine's most famous prayer as, 'Our hearts are restless until they find rest in thee.'[109] Vanhoozer describes humanity's essence as 'constituted by a desire for what is greater than itself, for ultimate reality',[110] ie for God. The limitations of Augustine's approach, however, lie in a particular theological assumption: 'Augustine turned inward because he was convinced that the inward journey marks the pathway to God.'[111] This was in turn founded upon Greek dualism, which promoted 'soul' over 'body' and so relegates concrete relatedness and direct encounter with others as a means of knowing God. This latter dimension can be argued to offer explanatory power as to how the human will (desire) is influenced and 'compelled',' 'co-created', as in McFadyen's case studies on sexual abuse and the Holocaust. Speaking of our 'willing' McFadyen writes:

> *This personal energy is not directed by the power of a pure, autonomous self. Willing is rather situated and relational, influenced in its orientation by extra – and supra – personal fields of force within one's situation. Through willing we incorporate ourselves into, internalise and redouble dynamics which are generally supra-personal and not of our own making, whilst adding our own personal power to them.*[112]

Godly pursuit, however, is not straightforward due to the effect of what Augustine regarded as original sin. This was seen as universal, and disempowering, causing humanity to pursue 'lesser goods' which would not satisfy in a deep or lasting way. The term concupiscence is used to denote this inordinate 'thirst' or perversion of what was initially created good – a desire for God. According to Pannenberg, a social dimension to original sin has always been present amidst the prophets of the Old Testament. This aspect which McFadyen also articulates enables an explanation of health which is socially and developmentally sensitive, yet preserves the individual as 'actor', initiator and responsible to use his or her will morally.

The principle of concupiscence lies at the heart of Hughes' model, as is evidenced by the importance given to Jeremiah 2:12–13 where, via the prophet, God questions His people as to why they have turned away from Him, the source of living water, and 'dug their own cisterns, broken cisterns that cannot hold water' (v13). Hughes, along with Augustine, would explain Israel's behaviour in terms of sin and its impact: idolatrous, disorientated desire. The Waverley Model Trainers' Notes also focus on another illustration of this principle. God speaks through Isaiah (55:1–2) inviting all, where awareness of 'thirst' is acknowledged, to turn from their natural disordered desire (spending money on what is not 'bread', labouring for that which will not satisfy), and turn to him for 'wine' and 'milk', without cost, which will satisfy. Motyer refers to the prior fruitless behaviour as arising from 'lack of discernment' and 'mental delusion'. Motyer regards bread, wine and milk as symbolically denoting every possible need, where 'every' is in context interpreted as spiritual. In this manner, Motyer gives deeper theological weight to the emphasis of the Waverley Model.

The implications for healthy functioning rooted in our God relationship are summarised by the Waverley Model as follows:

> *When we become dependent on someone else other than God for the meeting of our basic or crucial spiritual needs, we fall into the sin of idolatry – putting someone or something else in the place of God. True maturity of the personality can only come as we link ourselves to the resources which God has provided for the healthy functioning of the personality, for 'maturity', as someone said, is where you place your dependency.*[113]

The sin of idolatry is a broad biblical theme, and so the Waverley Model's emphasis on God dependence as primary for healthy functioning is a laudable one. However, the danger of this rightful emphasis is that it could be construed as conveying an absolute 'all or nothing' choice, if taken to an extreme, setting up an unhelpful polemic – a choice between God – or other-dependency. The subtext could be read as this: 'If we are fully dependent on God for our spiritual needs, we will be impervious to social conditions.' The corollary also follows: 'If we are deeply affected by circumstances then we probably are not dependent enough on God.' Such a perspective does not allow for how God may mediate His presence through family and culture, and thus gives no room for 'common grace', ie the awareness that others beyond the Church may represent the resources that God has provided. As Niebuhr puts it: 'the world of culture – man's achievement – exists within the world of grace – God's kingdom.'[114] This issue of 'wisdom theology' is explored in the next chapter (Model of Health).

Baxter, Scougal and motivation

It has been noted that during the Reformation Augustine's ideas were revitalised by, amongst others, Calvin and Luther. Richard Baxter is one example of a reformed Puritan pastor who utilised an approach to 'counselling' rooted in the premise that most problems stemmed from concupiscence (disoriented desire). Regarding Baxter's method Roth states:

> *His goal was to move the counselee away from dysfunctional living: that is, seeking to satisfy sinful drives (Rom. 6:12; James 1:14– 15), towards seeking happiness in the One who truly can satisfy the heart – God Himself (Rom. 6:11; Psa. 37:4; Matt. 5:6).[115]*

According to Baxter, this inward 'revolution' is the starting point of all godly change, and so is of primary focus in his method. Packer, who wrote his doctorate on Baxter's doctrine of humanity, speaks of Baxter's influence on other Christian leaders including John Wesley in the eighteenth century, Charles Spurgeon and Francis Asbury ('the Methodist apostle of America') in the nineteenth century. Roth argued that Puritans like Baxter believed original sin distorted motivation and hence the direction chosen in order to obtain wish fulfilment and thus satisfaction of desire. This pervasive view of corruption led Puritans (as did Augustine) to rely heavily on revealed truth (viewed as incorrupt due to a 'high' doctrine of inspiration) in Scripture as a means of transformation to health. This is clearly paralleled by Hughes' view of Scripture (see Chapter 1). In the context of ministry, Baxter's ideas regarding truth are clear; speaking of Scripture he states: 'The wisdom of the world must not be magnified against the wisdom of God, philosophy must be taught to swoop and serve, while faith doth bear the chief sway.'[116]

A contemporary of Baxter, Henry Scougal, also emphasised the necessity of inner renewal of desire by revelation of God's Spirit as the only means to true happiness and 'health'. The theme already articulated by Hughes, Crabb, Augustine and Baxter, runs through the 'core' of Scougal's anthropology:

> *Again, as divine love doth advance and elevate the soul; so it is*
> *that alone can make it happy; the highest and most ravishing*
> *pleasures; the most solid and substantial delights that human*
> *nature is capable of, are those which arise from the endearments of*
> *a well-placed and successful affection.*[117]

The converse is equally portrayed – love as a central human desire can become destructive when it is looking elsewhere for satisfaction: 'To all these evils are they exposed whose chief and supreme affection is placed on creatures like themselves, but the love of God delivers us from them all.'[118] The 'inward' emphasis within the Waverley Model abides amidst long-standing and diverse Christian traditions. Scougal's notion of true religion comprising an inward affective love of God has been regarded as having a vast legacy. Packer, declares it to have been 'favourite reading in Oxford's Holy Club' where Whitfield and the Wesleys first met. Scougal was part of what some scholars have referred to as the 'devotional revival' which, according to Packer also included Puritans like Perkins, Baxter and Owen; Anglicans like Jeremy Taylor; the Lutheran Johannes Arndt; and Roman Catholics like Ignatius Loyola, Francis de Sales, Teresa of Avila, and John of the Cross. Whilst it has been established that an emphasis on inwardness within the Church goes back as far as Augustine (and Pauline theology – although this is debated) it is interesting to note that the people listed lived during the Enlightenment, and so it could be argued that their subjective emphases reflect the tendency toward inwardness of this movement. Crabb and Hughes inherit this with the resultant marginalisation of identifying the self as socially embedded and shaped. Dyke asserts that the social self-predominated thinking from Socrates until the Enlightenment.

Critiquing inwardness – implications for therapy

Having sketched a historical outline of a theological tradition, which emphasises inwardness when defining personhood, Gunton's critique needs to be taken seriously as it has implications at both a personal and an ecological level. This helps keep in balance a view of personhood, for which this book is arguing – both substance and relationship are necessary constituents of personhood. Gunton states:

> *In particular, it encourages the belief that we are more minds than we are bodies, with all the consequences that has: for example, in creating a non-relational ontology, so that we are cut off from each other and the world by a tendency to see ourselves as imprisoned in matter.*[119]

After reviewing several approaches to the issue of personhood McFarlane's conclusion has a concrete and holistic tone. He states:

> *Whatever we say about the human person, it must dialogue with the present condition, individually and socially, politically and economically, not one abstracted to the historical past, teleological future or autonomous ego.*[120]

McFarlane's model focuses on Jesus, whose incarnation elevates bodiliness to primary importance, and thus helpfully guards against the historical temptation outlined above to relegate our bodily nature to secondary importance, as if it were a reluctant 'add on' or a secondary issue to relationship. Divine-human connection centred on Christ avoids an abstracted relationality argued from the immanent (God with Himself outside of relationship with the created order) Trinity, and instead portrays 'the image' from the human realm: 'centred on the embodied obedience of Jesus Christ whose personhood is displayed within this set of relationships, this exercise of power, this political and economic agenda.'[121] Christ becomes our integration point, the one who brings together the immanent and transcendent, the visible and invisible; the spiritual and material, the individual and social. Christ's call to follow Him (Mark 8:34 and Luke 9:23) and His own obedience to God (from childhood onwards), open up the realm of power in relationships and role modelling which all persons are subject to from birth. These provide the context out of which our wills operate, and through which we develop as persons; a dialogue (call and response) connects our becoming truly human to 'the other'. Smail explains the balance in this process which is necessary in order to give due weight to 'the other', yet retain the functioning of human agency. He states:

> *Even when we are most aware of the faceless forces that determine us, we never entirely lose the awareness that we are not passive objects at their mercy but active subjects with minds to comprehend what is happening to us and to determine our responses to it and with wills to intervene at some point in the causal chain of events and take action to move them in the direction we intend.*[122]

Distorted identity rooted in destructive patterns from the past can be reconfigured through new and different sets of relationships modelled on Christ. Christ's 'Kingdom come' not only becomes the centre for renewed minds and bodies, but also for renewed culture and environment, as the ultimate outworking of Christ's incarnation is a renewed heaven and earth. Thus, all these realms become a legitimate focus for change and may need to be considered within the counselling endeavour beyond the internal dynamic of the individual.

With regard to Hughes' focus for change, the starting point of creation and the Fall shapes his view of human nature. He focuses on a relationship with God which he describes pre-Fall as perfect, yielding a perfect sense of security, self-worth and significance, which represent Hughes' view of our core needs and identity. This particular portrayal does provoke questions as to how the Fall could occur under these circumstances. If our core longings (needs) are met in God alone, logically there would be no requirement to explain how temptation occurred, unless alongside our core longings there are other factors at work which Satan exploited. In contrast to Hughes' model of restoring the 'image' lost in the Fall, others interpret the Fall through an evolutionary lens. In this scheme humanity, as represented by Adam and Eve, did not originate in a perfect relationship with God, but rather one being transformed into a higher state of being – the Fall symbolises the emergence of sin as moral consciousness develops ; a fall 'upward' not 'downward'. Tennant states:

> *Man fell, according to science, when he first became conscious of the conflict of freedom and conscience. To the evolutionist, sin is not an innovation, but it is survival or misuse of habits that were incidental to an earlier stage of development.*[123]

This perspective brings to 'centre stage' a positive outlook on human potential; it emphasises possible progress and development as opposed to past omissions, deficits and their resultant guilt and responsibility.

The implications for counselling are significant, as problems may then be re-cast as opportunities for development of new patterns of thinking and relating. A further issue at stake for counselling regards the difficulty Hughes' model has in accounting for individual differences of dysfunction when in Hughes' account we have all suffered the same Fall, the same dislocation from God. Why does one person hold a belief that to be secure and feel good is fostered by dominating others, whilst another person may pursue the same goal by avoidance and withdrawal from those who are perceived to threaten security? A generic explanation is offered by Hughes, one rooted in the desire for independence from God, and our belief that we can make it work. Beyond this general disposition to self-deception, specific variations in the content of belief held by individuals are not accounted for. As mentioned earlier, a developmental perspective is alluded to: our deep longings are worked out in the first three years of life related to Erikson's first three psycho-social stages. This implies specific relational patterns impacting the emerging sense of self for each individual. A detailed account of this process could yield explanations particular to an individual's developmental pathway their unique and particular sets of relations against which they willed and responded. Here again, a model of personality will need to be open ended, emphasising the historic and ongoing impact of the outside conditions upon the 'inside' self (our core identity). McFadyen refers to this process as one of 'sedimentation', defined as follows:

> *The process by which a personal identity is accumulated by a significant history of address and response that has flowed around a particular point location and gathered around it in a unique way, so structuring a uniquely centred personal identity.*[124]

A focus on other genres of Scripture (beyond the Genesis creation narratives) gives additional weight to the enduring impact of external social conditions upon the personality, for example, Proverbs 22:6: 'Start children off on the way they should go, and even when they are old they will not turn from it.'[125] Waltke asserts that the thrust of this text is that: 'The consequences of this strong spiritual initiative are that the dedicated child will never depart from the original initiative.'[126] Also Proverbs 22:15; 23:13; 29:15 give similar weight to the relevance of social relationships in shaping personality development. In drawing the above issues together and in particular holding in balance 'call' and 'response' from both a spiritual and socially developmental perspective, we may arrive at a model of personality with the broadest explanatory power. This is a model which makes sense of both the metanarrative of Scripture (from Genesis to Revelation), with its themes of creation, the Fall, redemption etc, yet can embrace the particularity of an individual's response to both their developmental history and ongoing conditions. These themes may be symbolised via the adaptation of the Waverley Model's diagram for which this book argues.

Summary and evaluation

In answer to the question posed at the beginning of this chapter, 'Is the model clear yet comprehensive?' it has been demonstrated via contemporary (Crabb) and historical (Augustine and others) comparisons that the Waverley Model has a clear rationale rooted in a long-standing theological tradition.

However, from a relational standpoint, the model struggles to be deemed comprehensive as it does not give due weight to systemic and contextual factors, which alongside a person's unique responses explain individual differences. The relational deficit, as suggested, requires an adaptation of the traditional Waverley Model which can then portray persons as more dialogical, subject to variations of inter-relational dynamics. The way forward is not to deny the substantive emphasis upon individual interiority, but to place it in clear dialogue with the 'outside world'. Such a balance may be summed up by Vitz's theological formula of human ontology – 'substance and relationship' or 'relational substance'. Harris encapsulates an emphasis on this balance as follows:

> *I prefer to think of social and relational life as a continuum of interacting embodied subjectivities… we are moving away from the body as machine and towards a more plastic and complex 'body', where inside and outside fold around each other and distinctions like inside and outside are abstractions.*[127]

In the light of the above issues, Hughes' inward-focused holism will need to be augmented via a broader horizon – a holism which encompasses internal and external connectedness, such as that asserted by Richards and Bergin.

Chapter 3

Model of Health

In the preface to Christ *Empowered Living*, Selwyn Hughes outlines eight key issues which form the basis of his book. His model of health refers to wellbeing in general; of these key issues several are particularly significant for his model, which centres on relationship to God. He states:

> *The life behind and within the universe is the life of a God who is good and who has our highest interests at heart... We are built to relate first to Him and then to others... All spiritual/psychological problems have a relational component to them... Our problems can be resolved and overcome only when we decide to put Christ where He belongs – at the centre.*[128]

In the light of the above, it is unsurprising that the concept of repentance is explained as the key means through which health may be found. For Hughes, health has been undermined by sin, defined in essence as God-displacement. Thus a radical turn to God in dependent faith is key for Hughes' notion of healthy personality. Given the importance of this issue, it is necessary to discuss the concept of repentance further. Before doing this it is helpful to note that, for Hughes, repentance is not the only issue relevant to good health. Personal problems and their solutions are acknowledged as multiple. In addition, Hughes acknowledges that other people are a source of support and help. This theme of 'other-helping' is not developed beyond such allusions, perhaps as a product of Hughes' desire to put God-dependency at the centre of his teaching. This emphasis may also arise out of his definition of sin as God-displacement. A further cause may link to the model's Augustinian roots where finding God within us de-emphasises finding God in others. Such views can offer an explanation as to why Hughes does not develop a theology regarding how God may be mediated through the Church, other people and the world in general. A further factor is the consequence of classical evangelicalism (Hughes' formative context) and its over-emphasis on the God–self relationship at the expense of the God–neighbour relationship.

Repentance

Repentance is an important biblical concept. The most common term for repentance *shub* in the Old Testament occurs over a thousand times, and is translated 'repent' or 'repentance', however, most commonly in the New International Version it is 'turn' or 'return'. A second term is *naham* which expresses both a cognitive and affective component – sorrow, lament, grief and a change of mind. In view here is a turning from evil and a turning to good. Volf defines the process as a profound moral and religious turnaround. The inclusion of 'religious' helps keep the biblical context of relationship to God as opposed to any turnabout. Of critical importance theologically is the turning to God, which by definition involves turning away from evil. In the Old Testament, this call to turn is largely found in the prophets and applied to Israel corporately, and so can be understood in terms of the covenant obligation to reflect God.

In the New Testament, the call to repentance becomes individual, yet universal via the Church's call to mission (Matt. 28:18–20). Both Mark (1:15) and Matthew (4:17) start Jesus' public proclamations with the call 'Repent'. The key Greek word for repentance is metanoia, which Dunnet claims has two senses – a change of mind and an affective sense of remorse or regret. Adams, however, focuses exclusively on the cognitive when defining repentance, arguing that affective elements will be part of the overall experience, but are in fact a consequence to rethinking our attitudes and behaviours. His definition emerges from his understanding of the Greek term metanoia. He states:

*There's nothing in the word metanoia about sorrow; indeed it
does not mention the emotions at all. That is not to say that true
repentance will not lead to sorrow, but the word itself carries no
such connotation.*[129]

Verbrugge agrees with Adams' rendering of metanoia, but asserts that the
overall experience will involve an emotion of (amongst others) joy. This is
because repentance is linked to the promise of new life. Verbrugge further
helps us grasp the broad Scriptural presentations of the concept of repentance
by making clear that whilst the grouped words, *metanoeo* and *epistrepho* occur
only six times in Paul's letters and none in John's writings, the central idea is
conveyed via different imagery. Paul uses several terms: 'in Christ', 'dying
and rising', 'new creation', 'putting on the new self'. John uses 'new birth',
'passing from death to life', 'darkness to light', and the 'victory of truth over
falsehood', and 'love over hate'.

Whilst there are different interpretations of the key Greek word metanoia,
the broader biblical evidence points to a more holistic process than merely a
change of mind, although how we delineate the concept and its consequences
is crucial in this respect. Repentance is not merely a cognitive measure, but is
represented in Scripture as involving the whole person (Matt. 3:8 and Mark
10:21). We can conclude then that repentance is at the heart of a Christian
world-view of health, as it is foundational to the gospel of salvation (Hebrews
6:1). This expectation is part of the tension of the 'now' and 'not yet' – the
'end-time' fullness already in process of becoming present reality. Thus for
Paul and the initial recipients of Romans, salvation and life were virtually
synonymous. In its broadest sense, the power of God for salvation (Rom.
1:16) is used to refer to both justification and sanctification. It follows that the
rest of Romans expand upon these concepts one from the other; chapters one
to five explain the need for and means of obtaining our justification, chapters
six to eight and twelve to fifteen, the experience of sanctification. Hill refers
to the relational dynamics of salvation righteousness as both establishing us
(justifying) and equipping us as covenant partners, with the power to relate
in a manner which reflects God as righteous, ie God both forgives and is in
the ongoing business of converting (transforming). Dunn crystallises Paul's

thoughts regarding the phrase 'the power of God for salvation' as denoting: 'a force that operates with marked effect on people, transforming them… and providing a source of energy to sustain that qualitatively different life.'[130]

If notions of transformation are implicit in salvation (albeit there are differing views as to how much change can be expected in this life), then the means of bringing about such change is, for Paul, located in offering oneself to God in acts of worship, coupled with a renewing of our minds. Indeed, the exhortations found in Romans 12:1–2 are pivotal in the structure of Paul's letter and are founded upon the previous eleven chapters. Admittedly, the biblical connection between doctrine and daily living is to be expected, given the context of a Jewish world-view. Jesus thus taught: 'Now that you know these things, you will be blessed if you do them' (John 13:17). Paul, in other letters, also often follows a doctrinal exposition with an ethical exhortation (Eph. 4:1; Col. 3:5). Commenting on Romans 12:1–2, Barth also emphasises the 'now' element of these exhortations: 'Our conversation is about men living in the world of nature and of civilisation; and, moreover, we ourselves are also men living of necessity from minute to minute a quite concrete life.'[131]

The exhortation 'offer your bodies' (Rom. 12:1), is in context used to mean person, our whole selves, not just in individual isolation but in concrete relatedness within the world. Thus it is through our bodiliness that we relate to others and express the life that is in us; either imaging God and so reaping life and health, or distorting this image in sinful patterns which ultimately lead to pathology and eternal death. In this way, Paul's exhortation to 'offer our bodies' can be seen as an invitation to reconfigure the patterns of relationships which have previously shaped our identities. From this viewpoint a 'turnaround' in transforming ourselves is therefore synonymous with transforming relationships. This offers a theological means by which we may make sense of Hughes' statement quoted at the beginning of this chapter: 'All spiritual/ psychological problems have a relational component.'[132]

Due in part to the tension of the 'already' and the 'not yet' context of God's kingdom in which we live, the call to be transformed is not without resistance and struggle, as the world exerts a continual pull to mould us into its patterns of relatedness and subsequent identity. From a Pauline perspective, the means by which we may enter, endure, and triumph over such a struggle is by the continual 'renewing of our minds' (Rom. 12:2). The term 'renewal of minds' to Paul has a dualistic connotation; it includes one's body (relationships to the world as discussed earlier) as there is no body/mind dualism in Paul's thought.

In the counselling context a central facet of living in wholeness involves the 'renewing of our minds'. The importance of the impact a person's uniquely individual thinking has on their health is generally agreed among Christian and non-Christian approaches alike. Developmentally, from age four to five, a person will be able to construct beliefs about themselves that markedly differ from the evaluation of others, for example, how popular we are. In narrative therapy terms, the repetitions of destructive relational patterns are regarded as arising out of family generated 'myths' or 'scripts' or ideas about the self and the world. This perspective is helpful in pointing out the context within which we need to understand pathology or health. The family, for instance, can foster what might be regarded as realistic and healthy 'scripts' or the converse.

For Christians, this kind of insight links healthy personality to 'true family' or 'community', and in particular openness to the person or persons within such corporate structures who set the agendas that foster true identity. Most helpful in this regard is a model of imago Dei which focuses on Christ as 'fully human', whose pattern we can internalise and imitate. As McFadyen puts it:

> *In Christian tradition, Christ is the concrete history*
> *wherein God's call and human response are present together.*
> *His individual identity... together with the content of his*
> *communication therefore has a normative status[133]*

Thus, Christ is the agent who makes our transformative salvation realisable in concrete 'here and now' relatedness and gives rise to the general declaration of John 10:10, 'I have come that they may have life, and have it to the full.' The imagery used of a shepherd and his sheep has the connotation. This includes the notion of God's provision of care and safety as he looks after 'his sheep'; which stands in contrast to the 'thieves and robbers' (v1). The implicit challenges of experiencing health are introduced elsewhere through the extension of the above imagery (Matt. 7:15, wolves in sheep's clothing). In utilising shepherd imagery in the way He does, Jesus personalises the Old Testament expectation of God becoming Israel's Shepherd in the future (Isa. 40:11; Jer. 31:10; Ezek. 34:11–16).

Different imagery is used elsewhere in John's Gospel to convey the same principle of health (wholeness) in relationship to Christ. For example, John 6:32–40 (true bread from heaven), 15:1 (the true vine) – the former we need to internalise (eat); the latter we need to ensure we are a part of (connected to). So in 14:6–7 Jesus can claim to be 'the way and the truth and the life'.[134]

The varied and extensive use of the above kind of imagery offers a clear principle that health or wholeness is firmly linked to a God relationship, and so endorses Hughes' Christ-centred emphasis. This most clearly applies to those in covenant relationship – in the Old Testament, the nation of Israel; in the New Testament, Christians. The issue therefore arises as to how those outside such a covenant experience health. In the context of the Waverley Model, the specific question arises: Does this Christ-centred model apply to those who are not Christians? Can the Waverley Model offer any accounts as to why in general terms non-Christians can live healthy and productive lives?

Repentance and wisdom

Niebuhr provides a helpful framework for discussing the issues of salvific and common wisdom. The perspectives utilised in answering the questions being posed will have significant overlap with the views discussed in Chapter 1 (see 'Relating Theology and Psychology '), where four differing views as to the relationship between special and common revelation were discussed. As a general starting point and summary of a perspective for which this book argues, Niebuhr's comments are helpful: 'The Christian life moves between the poles of God in Christ as known through faith and the Bible and God in nature as known through reason in culture.'[135]

The culturally embedded human production of knowledge via reason, science etc is coincident with faith and so forms part of its referent, ie the two means of knowing (faith and science) correlate to some degree and so cannot be seen as totally exclusive or absolute alternatives. An understanding that Christ is the foundation of both faith and reason (salvation and wisdom) provides a general theological bridge which connects these two domains.

For Niebuhr, both faith and reason are mediated – the former via the Church and our culturally embedded theological and spiritual practices; the latter via our social, political and economic structures which may communicate God's truth by greater or lesser degrees, for example, individuals treated with a dignity that reflects humanity made in God's image. To the degree that this occurs, the Church will provide support for these practices; in contexts where such values are not held and practised, the Church can provide a voice of protest. The theological category of 'Natural Law' helps express the idea of the convergence of faith and reason. It claims that certain truths and behaviours transcend the variations of culture, as they match up (albeit unwittingly) to God's Eternal Law in the creation order, and so are inherently stable and if adhered to, promote healthy living. Commenting on the prologue in John's Gospel (John 1:1–8), Ford, looking for wisdom beyond Scripture (which for him is still central) cites the whole of creation as the wisdom context, and so concludes that 'nothing in principle can be ruled out as relating to Scripture and its understanding, and hence to Christ'.[136]

Beasley-Murray and Bennema confirm the theological importance of John's prologue in contrast to Luke's prologue. They believe the former sets the context for understanding the whole of John's Gospel. This confirms the relationship of Christ (the Logos) to creation as a significant theological theme, as opposed to a prologue as 'mere introduction' prior to the 'main event'. Verse four of John's prologue establishes Christ not only as mediator of the creation historically, but also of His continuous sustaining of creation.

Christ is theologically the one who thus 'holds all things together'– special and general revelation. Christ's rule, whilst most explicit in the Church (Eph. 4), can also be manifest generally in societies which display His 'kingdom rule.' Middleton argues the case for this latter manifestation to be regarded as the creative outworking of a functional interpretation of imago Dei (Gen. 1:28) where humanity continues God's creative work of 'forming' and 'filling' the earth. Middleton points out that in Genesis 1, God's creative act is developmental and transformative. Human activity likewise may be worked out in transforming culture and developing civilisation. The specific human task of Genesis 2:15 ('till' and 'keep' the garden) may be viewed as a paradigmatic agricultural metaphor understood as 'transform' and 'organise'. These innate ongoing (post-Fall) human capacities are highlighted within the wisdom literature of Scripture, where it is assumed that through experience and education wisdom may be gained. Furthermore, the implications of wisdom Christology are that this wisdom will be encountered in what is lived (embodied), as much, if not more than in what is communicated linguistically (verbal or written). Consequently Paul appeals to the Corinthians to imitate what they see in his life (1 Cor. 4:16; 11:1). Biblical wisdom also requires the use of reason and discernment to interpret wisdom, rather than blind obedience. This implies God's wisdom is not procedurally straightforward as in the discovery of a rule for every situation; this is because God's wisdom is both authoritative and cognitive in nature. This requires obedience to principles clearly revealed which relate to health or pathology, yet also a responsibility to work at understanding how life and the world are organised. Thus speaking of biblical wisdom Schnabel states:

> *Israelite sages sought to understand how life and the world worked, asking questions which today are part of scientific inquiry and philosophical reflection; inquiry into the animate and inanimate world[137]*

Wisdom aligns human flourishing within a context of the social and the creation order. Having said this, we may avoid the idea that such wisdom is simply grasped by autonomous human reason (natural theology) as Paul's critique of the latter makes clear (1 Cor. 1:18–2:16). Ford ultimately asserts an inherent tension between God-centred wisdom and human derived wisdom, but regards Luke's Gospel in particular as encouraging, even demanding a pursuit of commonly available wisdom. His analysis of Luke 11:27–32 and especially verse 31 (Jesus' exaltation of the 'Queen of the South' for seeking Solomon's wisdom) gives rise to an exhortation to be like the queen in having an openness to learn from others 'beyond your usual horizons' (implying for evangelical Christians beyond Scripture and Christian theology). Others offer alternative emphases from this passage suggesting the real focus is Jesus, the 'true wisdom'. Lastly, in trying to balance a Christ-centred focus with generally available wisdom, Ford states:

> *The queen is not likely to be the only witness at the judgment to accuse you of failing to attend to wisdom: think who the other witnesses down through the centuries might be, then try to learn what they learnt – above all what they learnt about Jesus, but also like Solomon, about the cosmos, nature, family, society, ethics, politics, economics, education, God and love.*[138]

Such a perspective has its critics, founded on the fear (and they would add clear evidence) that common wisdom, as seen through a 'kingdom perspective', inevitably becomes, not an adjunct to but rather an opponent, and ultimately a usurper of biblical truth. The Bobgans put it as follows with regard to the contemporary counselling context:

> *More and more Christians are looking to psychologists as though they are the wise men of the twentieth century. Psychologists have taken the position of priests and have replaced the pastors as 'experts' in all matters pertaining to life. Freud and Jung et al speak for us instead of the apostles and prophets.*[139]

Adams is quite clear about the fact that the issues with which people now attend counselling are generally the same ones for which they used to seek out the pastor – issues of belief, attitude, value, behaviour, relationship etc. With regard to being a competitor to a biblical world-view rooted in Scripture, Adams does delineate between general medicine and academic psychology on the one hand, which he regards as having an ancillary role, as opposed to psychiatry and clinical/counselling psychology on the other hand, which according to Adams have illegitimately set themselves up as competitors. Adams is adamant that Christian counselling should not be dependent upon data from these latter two fields of knowledge. This is because Adams on the whole regards the likes of Freud, Rogers and Skinner as setting up rival not ancillary perspectives. He appears to give little if any room to wisdom beyond Scripture. Citing Genesis 3 and Psalm 1 as evidence, he categorises knowledge into two parts: Godly – almost exclusively restricted to Scripture – and satanic, concluding there is no warrant for a third 'neutral counsel'. He does discuss the notion, 'All truth is God's truth' under the category of 'common grace' but only to assert that the ideas of Freud etc cannot represent this commonly available truth. This is argued on two grounds: firstly, that God would never set up rival systems of counsel to the Bible; secondly, that God does not duplicate in general revelation what He has already revealed in Scripture.

Adams' argument, unfortunately, does not stand up to scrutiny; Freud, for example, only becomes a rival system if we accept all his ideas. However, it is quite possible to embrace aspects of his work on defence mechanisms, for example, the heart's propensity to self-deception (Jer. 17:9), and hence the scriptural imperative to examine ourselves as a guard against such deceit, for example, Psalm 139:23–4 and 2 Corinthians 13:5–9. Freud's work on ego defences can thus be viewed (as Adams would approve) as ancillary – a filling out of a biblical theme. At the same time, we do not have to agree with Freud in his contention that God is in fact really a projection of a human father figure, though it is quite possible that our God-image in part is comprised of such projections.

Adams' second assertion of general and special revelation not being duplicated is contradicted by Psalm 19 and Romans 1, where the principle of duplication or 'mirroring' is central. Hence for Paul, no one has an excuse that they were not told about God's existence, as creation 'parallels' Christ in showing God's glory (Rom. 1:19–20).

In principle, therefore, the wisdom tradition offers a bridge to link Christ with elements of the created social order. Rather than adopt a 'Christ against culture' position (as Adams does), we can with discernment and judgment rooted in Scripture, develop a 'Christ in culture' position. Regarding the counselling process, the central activity of self-examination can lead to healthier patterns of living as clients move from defensive forms of identity to a more honest and realistic self-appraisal. Given the concept of sin as both individual and systemic (see Chapter 1, the 'Summary and Evaluation' of 'Sin') health-producing change will be limited if only seen from the perspective of the 'sinful soul'.

Such an emphasis alone has, as Volf puts it, 'served to divert attention from the economics of dirty deals and politics of ruthless power'.[140] Such structural sin which the Marxist tradition described must also be addressed. Biblical wisdom has been defined as: 'the ability to make Godly choices in life.'[141] Or in a fuller statement: 'prudent, considered, experienced and competent action to subjugate the world and to master the various problems in life.'[142] Honest self-appraisal is an aspect of God's wisdom found in the ethics of counselling. As McFarlane expresses, commenting on Proverbs 3:15f plus chapter eight, 'lady wisdom' brings benefits to all who seek her, for she shows how the world was made and promotes human agency (dominion) through its immanent goodness in creation. Human wisdom in society (mediated in cultural expressions, for instance elements of contemporary counselling) is judged by how it corresponds to the order of creation. Wisdom theology thus helps avoid an 'all or nothing' approach in counselling, ie 'unless clients accept Christ via repentance we can offer them nothing of value pertaining to health'. It is a lack of wisdom theology which compels Adams to adopt a simple biblical–satanic stance. Whereas Niebuhr's categories are helpful in highlighting the fact that Adam's position correlates with a 'Christ against culture' perspective, this is but one of several positions taken throughout Church history. Alternatively, a 'Christ in Culture' perspective gives rise to the expectation that God's truth and helpfulness may be encountered more broadly, thus for example, amidst elements of secular counselling.

Repentance and counselling

Within the context of counselling the means by which healthy living may be obtained is, in principle varied and creative. This expectation mirrors the various forms of scriptural wisdom and includes close observations of life, which support scientifically based methods such as CBT; or alternatively, storytelling and dialogue, which aligns with narrative and person-centred therapeutic approaches. Wisdom's manifold forms are well summed up by Deane-Drummond who, when citing the Apocrypha states: 'Wisdom is intelligent, holy, unique, manifold, subtle, mobile, incisive, unsullied, lucid, invulnerable, benevolent, beneficent friendly to human beings'

(Wisdom 7:22–23).[143] An approach to God's truth derived from wisdom is thus dialogical, and open ended, embracing new dialogue partners as new disciplines and new data emerge. It encapsulates something similar to what Webb calls a 'redemptive–movement hermeneutic'.[144] This aims at apprehending the 'spirit' of Scripture relating to God's universal wisdom that can then be reapplied in new contexts. This approach also recognises that Scripture as a whole does not offer a stationary ethic but one that develops through its pages and in principle is still developing today. Its spirit can be worked out and applied in the light of the current cultural and scientific context. Webb alternatively calls his approach a 'progressive', 'developmental' or 'trajectory' interpretive method. He explains further that an understanding of God's wisdom means Scripture functions in a way that moves us toward a redemptive goal, accommodating our need to grow and develop within cultural contexts. He states:

> *Both the divine and human authors function together in a gentle,*
> *pastoral relationship to the covenant community... Their words are*
> *designed to 'stretch' the covenant people as far as they could go,*
> *like an elastic band, but not to cause them to 'snap'.[145]*

When considering the above points it is possible to realise that cultural conditions change; such an approach could embrace the redemptive interpretive ethic and thereby foster a climate of health in a manner that was not realised in the past.

It is possible that certain elements in the counselling process such as mercy and honesty embody redemptive ethics and thereby promote health. McMinn calls this 'interpersonal redemption', which people can offer each other as they model healthy relationships as viewed from a biblical perspective. In concrete terms, what this 'redemption' looks like will vary from case to case; for example, someone born into abusive relational systems may not have learned appropriate self-care and assertion of related boundaries, which could be modelled and learnt through the counselling relationship. Alternatively, someone who has been the perpetrator of abusive domineering styles of relating, perhaps as a defence against an internal sense of vulnerability and weakness, can be helped through a counsellor's feedback and modelling, to learn to acknowledge and deal with inferiority in new ways, and hence be freed to foster a more empathetic and other-centred style of life.

Both biblical wisdom and some major counselling theories affirm the need to grow into maturity. Both acknowledge the crucial role of relationships in developing this maturity. Both avoid 'quick-fix' mentality. Having used the Bible's concept of wisdom in fostering openness to learning about health from non-biblical sources (science and culture) a cautionary note is warranted. Whilst wisdom is 'the search to discover the inter-relationships of everything',[146] judgment is required regarding which secular insights will be consistent with our biblical world-view and values, and which may undermine them – like Adams' 'competitors'. To miss this latter possibility is to ignore a doctrine of sin and fail to recognise what Johnson referred to as a 'kingdom' element in the production of knowledge (see Chapter 1). Anderson warns of a creeping syncretism that he asserts has done the most damage to the worldwide Church. The various warnings in Scripture validate, in general terms, Anderson's concern. They moderate and qualify a wisdom call to embrace what the world can offer, by focusing upon the potential conflicts. The Bible uses various images to convey this principle, including a promise of life which turns out to be death (2 Cor. 11:13–15); health that turns out to be pathology; a 'wolf in sheep's clothing' (Matt. 7:15); and the world as an enemy of God (James 4:4). Anderson further enlarges a conflict model by citing Galatians 5:17 where Paul establishes the opposition of the sinful nature (Greek *sarx*, KJB 'flesh') to the spirit.

In Chapter 1 it was argued that a biblical theology of the doctrine of sin included both individual and systemic (including social and cosmic) aspects. This concept of sin when applied to counselling theories necessitates a scrutiny of all secular theories, so as to identify possible ideas, values and practices that oppose those of Scripture, whilst at the same time welcoming elements that are consistent with and further illuminate a biblical stance.

Although 'all truth is God's truth',[147] it is equally true that due to the distorting power of sin not all that sets itself up as true and life-giving actually ends up as such. Having argued for a position of careful integration the question remains: how do we delineate the good and healthy from the not so good and unhealthy?

Being open to the findings of science but desiring to evaluate them from a biblical world-view, both Crabb and Hughes adopt a 'spoiling the Egyptians' method. Both however have a strong focus on the Bible's ability to render a model of health as it explicitly reveals Christ as the ultimate wisdom – 'the way and the truth and the life' (John 14:6).

In Chapter 1, 'Image of God', it was argued that a biblical approach to understanding humanity emerges from a consideration of what is meant by the phrase 'made in God's image' and that the Waverley Model Trainers' Notes rightly emphasise this starting point in developing a doctrine of humanity. In a chapter entitled 'God's Perfect Man', Hughes sets forth Christ as our ultimate example of wisdom incarnate – the model of healthy living. Hughes asserts that, while the expression 'the image of God' occurs only once in the Old Testament after the creation account (Gen. 9:6); in the New Testament it appears several times. In 1 Corinthians 11:7, man is referred to as the 'image and glory of God'. In 2 Corinthians 4:4, 'image of God' is used to refer to Christ; in Colossians 1:15 and 3:10 Christ restores 'the image'. In Hebrews 1:3 Christ is declared to be the 'exact representation' of God's being (Greek *kharakter*). Dunn helps us connect Christ as 'the image' and notions of biblical wholeness (salvation). Christ succeeds where Adam (the first bearer of the image motif) failed: 'Paul describes man's salvation in many ways, using many metaphors. In particular he understands salvation as the fostering or reshaping of the believer into the image of God.'[148]

This reshaping most obviously occurs through repentance and an ongoing following (modelling) of Christ – 'the wisdom of God'. However, it also occurs as we are exposed to, and align ourselves with more commonly available wisdom – this is what Hughes refers to as 'lighthouse laws': He states:

*The laws of God both in the natural and spiritual spheres are
like lighthouses. They cannot shift and cannot change. As Cecil
B. De Mille observed in his film, The Ten Commandments,
'It is impossible for us to break laws, we only break ourselves
upon them.' The lighthouse laws that govern human growth and
happiness are woven into the fabric of our society and comprise
the roots of every family and institution that has endured and
prospered.[149]*

Despite a robust doctrine of sin, Hughes embraces a vestige of 'natural law' –
'He has in fact written his law twice, once in the text of the Bible and once in the
texture of human nature.'[150] So God's moral law is congruent with our 'created
being' and thus for Hughes, our 'true humanness' is experienced by obeying this
law – or to put it another way, we will enjoy health as we realign ourselves with
God's relational order as originally designed, His good creation. The biblical
concepts of creation, the Fall and Christ's inauguration of a new creation that is
still in process ('Your kingdom come') give rise to an awareness that the pursuit
of, and maintenance of health will include potential conflict and struggle – a
denial of immediate self-gratification in order to find a deeper spiritual self-
aligned to Christ likeness. In this light we can make sense of Christ's words:
'Whoever wants to be my disciple must deny themselves and take up their cross
daily and follow me. For whoever wants to save their life will lose it, but whoever
loses their life for me will save it' (Luke 9:23–24; Matt. 16:24–25; Mark 8:34–35).
This apparent paradox is clarified by Hughes when he asserts that the primary
issue pertaining to health is 'worship of God' (law 1). This is significant from
a psychological perspective as it links with an individual's ability to entrust
themselves to another – the healthy denial of oneself in order to pursue a God
relationship is foundational for healthy living. It has already been outlined that
trust in others, which is necessary to create a sense of security, is for Hughes the
first psychologically- and spiritually-oriented developmental challenge for any
human (see Chapter 2, 'Model of Personality'). It will be seen in the next chapter
how failure to successfully respond to this human necessity is at the heart of
many aspects of human pathology, both at a spiritual and psychological level.

Summary and evaluation

In this chapter it has been noted that for Hughes a relationship with God is regarded as essential for forming and sustaining a healthy personality. Sin is the overarching concept that is used to explain pathology (that which disrupts and militates against health). Other factors beyond personal sin are included, for example physical illness, bodily malfunctions and relationships with others. Despite awareness of these latter factors, sin (articulated as God-displacement) remains as a central feature which undermines healthy functioning, and therefore repentance is offered as the primary mechanism through which we may move towards health. Thus Hughes' overriding desire for everyone to turn to Christ in faith may have the effect of lessening awareness of how God can inhabit the world of culture and science, and how varying levels of health may be derived outside of an explicit 'turn to Christ'.

Theologically, it has been shown how a robust wisdom Christology provides a means through which health may be expected to flourish on the back of human learning and practices that by degrees may naturally align themselves with God's creation order. Ford, for example, can therefore claim that nothing in principle can be ruled out as having some connection to God's healing truth – Christ.

It was noted that biblical wisdom literature has a human-centred focus which emphasises human agency and learning, of itself generally beneficial to healthy living. Adams and the Bobgans hold a different perspective that allows only two categories of knowledge relating to health: Godly, almost exclusively scriptural, which yields healthy living; and demonic, most other forms of counsel. This position was critiqued on the grounds that it lacked engagement with a wisdom Christology and so evoked a narrow explanation of the means of health.

Wisdom Christology enables a more 'open-ended' view of where life-giving truth may be found than Adams and the Bobgans permit; Scripture can have many dialogue partners. One outworking of the above principle is Webb's 'redemptive hermeneutic' which engenders a view of truth that is progressive and to some extent flexible rather than static. Practically, this means that for counselling methods, new ideas can be incorporated and utilised creatively in accordance with the 'spirit of Scripture'. McMinn's concept of 'interpersonal redemption' captures something of how a counsellor's relational style may, for example, mediate Christ's grace and mercy; it thereby broadens our ideas of healing factors beyond the ethical imperatives of Scripture. Anderson, by drawing our attention to a 'conflict model' of human functioning rooted in Scripture, helpfully explains why obtaining health may involve struggle.

Lastly, Hughes' notion of 'lighthouse laws' embraces aspects of commonly available human wisdom as potentially health promoting. This distinguishes his approach from those like Adams', but his robust doctrine of sin entails the necessity of using discernment when utilising this imperfect wisdom. Thus, 'spoiling the Egyptians' is a phrase which gives Hughes a biblical warrant for capturing the balance of his approach.

Having outlined the parameters of Hughes' model of health, and explained how a wisdom Christology enables his Christ-centred approach to have relevance beyond the Christian community, it is now necessary to explore how those principles apply to the converse case of pathology. This is the theme of the following chapter – 'Model of Abnormality'.

Chapter 4

Model of Abnormality

Hughes' notion of health centres upon a specific understanding of the human relationship with God; namely:

> *We are built to relate first to Him and then to others. All spiritual/psychological problems have a relational component to them... Our problems can be resolved and overcome only when we decide to put Christ where He belongs – at the centre.*[151]

In light of the above it is not surprising that, for Hughes, a model of abnormality is theologically founded upon the impact of separation from God as articulated in the Fall narrative of Genesis chapter three. It has been stated that approaching personhood from a creation perspective fosters a relational focus of 'I–Thou' address, which takes us beyond mere historical curiosity regarding origins. It has already been outlined (Chapter 2, 'Model of Personality') as to how a relational emphasis sits well with the Waverley Model, although 'relational' is primarily to God via repentance. Broader relationships (culture, other humans, the environment) are marginalised in their significance for yielding either healthy or abnormal development. Emphasis on repentance emerges from a lack of engagement with a wisdom Christology, (see Chapter 3, 'Model of Health'). What follows is a brief outline of the Waverley Model's account of abnormality; from this a comparison and contrast may be made with several psychodynamic theorists – Freud, Fairbairn and Bowlby, who represent a range of emphases regarding relational and structural accounts of personhood.

The Waverley Model and Abnormality

The Waverley Model Trainers' Notes render a model of sin which is rooted in Adam's rebellion, articulated as being motivated by an unwillingness to trust God and His ethical imperatives as being life-giving. The relational dislocation in Eden is taken as paradigmatic, and this in principle explains all subsequent distortions of personhood:

> *Due to the Fall people are both dignified and depraved. The image of God has been defaced by depravity but it is still within us though broken, disfigured and fragmented. By 'depravity' we mean the violation of God's design through self-centredness and self-determination.*[152]

As dependent beings, critical needs were met through a God relationship, whereas after the Fall those needs were not fully satisfied. As a result, the three core needs (longings, desires) remained unfulfilled and so, in general terms, a capacity for security was experienced as insecurity; self-worth as inferiority; and significance as insignificance.

In the Waverley Model, the desire for satisfaction of core longings remains, despite its proper object of fulfilment (God) having been lost; from this arises a turn to 'other gods' – idols – in an attempt to find satisfaction and spiritual contentment. This is where the Waverley Model is most explicitly Augustinian in its theory of motivation. This has been discussed previously (see Chapter 2, 'Model of Personality'). In explaining this principle, Hughes gives a prominent place to Jeremiah 2:12–13 – God's indictment of Israel for 'digging broken cisterns'.[153] This image is of such importance to Hughes that it is worth scrutinising in some depth.

'Broken cisterns'

For Hughes, the behaviour in view – digging broken cisterns – is horrifying from a heavenly perspective; Jeremiah 2:12 says, 'Be appalled at this, you heavens, and shudder with great horror'. However, to Hughes this makes sense subjectively for Israel in so far as they believe that such a strategy will yield life, 'a distorted perception has arisen out of their remoteness from God'.[154] This situation does not seem to apply only to particular individuals or even only to this particular generation, and so taking it as paradigmatic likewise would appear reasonable. Furthermore, as Osborne points out, the function of the prophetic ministry was not so much innovation, but reformation: 'They applied the truths of the past to the nation's current situation... revivalists, seeking to bring the people back to Yahweh.'[155] From this perspective, the theme of Jeremiah 2 has a resonance with that of the Fall – the human tendency for self-determination and a corollary of destructive consequences (via God's judgment), in response to human independence which has disrupted the design of creation. Indeed, Fee and Stuart argue against such passages as Jeremiah 2 being read for detailed application ('bottom level') but rather that they be read from a metanarrative perspective ('top level') as their purpose is to illustrate amongst other things the Fall and the ubiquity of human sin.

The Waverley Model Trainers' Notes give prominence to Jeremiah 2:12–13 and other Scriptures (Isa. 55:1–2; Psa. 42:1; 143:6; Matt. 5:6; John 7:37) which establish core biblical themes of human existence, for instance spiritual longings which require satisfaction; being dependent on God and yet having a human propensity for self-determination. The importance of this stance has been argued elsewhere (see Chapter 2, 'Model of Personality'). However, the way the image of water is utilised in Jeremiah 2 is but one of three main usages throughout Scripture. God as provider of life giving 'water' connects to the resultant human necessity of obtaining a regular supply of this water in order to prevent breakdown of functioning in general. Hughes acknowledges that God mediates this supply of water beyond a direct personal 'turn to Christ in faith' – our spiritual longings, as Hughes defines them, are 'waiting to be filled by those who nurture us'.[156] Pannenberg also recognised that this is because basic trust is directed toward an agency that best fits the need for unlimited security and promotion of the self. The quality of nurture provided by the temporal object(s) will form a prototype of experience that will influence our later attachments (even to God). It follows that because the quality of nurturing care varies from person to person, so will its impact upon the infant's sense of security.

Alongside relational factors influencing the formation of self, Hughes also allows room for the contribution of individual response to this process (construction, evaluation, perception). This provides both an ethical basis for individual judgment by God and hope for change in so far as we were active participants in the development of pathology, and have likewise become active in creating a new sense of self and its consequent relational patterns. Pannenberg identifies with this balanced approach regarding responsibility for the development of self:

> *While the identity of individuals is not to be conceived as a product of a subject that already exists with its own identity, neither is it to be understood as a simple internalisation of social appraisals and expectations.*[157]

Like Pannenberg, Turner puts forward a view of self (both pathological and healthy) that is derived via a combination of individual (internal) and social (external) factors. For Turner, to ignore the sociological aspect of our understanding would dislocate our concepts of pathology and health from their 'social moorings', and also leave the concept of self reduced to modernity's autonomous ego, which he rightly asserts is now almost universally rejected. Equally perturbing for Turner would be a sole reliance on sociological (relational) explanations, as this would undermine the importance of an individual's psychological and biological processes in the construction of self. Additionally, Jewett adds theological weight to this perspective in his answer to the question of how we might understand the human self in the light of biblical revelation. His answer centres upon 'I' as an 'I' in relation to the 'other' (God and neighbour), yet this description depends upon the 'selves' being distinct – our humanity is given as individual persons. Thus, we may still be seen as discrete entities (uniquely individual and separate) but always existing in relational networks.

A model of self-development that is not purely 'external download' also gives explanatory space for individual difference, both at a micro level, for example, how children in a family, exposed to the same relational environment, can turn out to be different; and at a broader social level, for example, opposition to Hitler within Germany during the 1930s and 1940s. Hughes' focus on Israel's digging broken cisterns is an example of the outworking of what Kelsey explains as distorted identity rooted in optimism (our own resources will yield life in its fullness) as opposed to 'end times' hope which is rooted in God's promise of provision (water) for abundant life. Hughes' assertion regarding the human propensity for self-determination makes sense of Israel's corporate 'pathology'.

Abnormality and unmet deep longings

The Waverley Model Trainers' Notes state that behind most destructive behaviour patterns is an attempt to alleviate the deep pain of an unmet 'thirst' for security. The drive to find a secure foundation (accepting love) for our personal functioning is so critical to the Waverley Model's concept of motivation that it is worth exploring this phenomenon in some depth. In particular, the above explanation of development opens up an inquiry into how Christ may mediate our personal and cultural experiences by varying degrees, depending on the extent to which they mirror His created design.

The theme of human attachment in Scripture has been widely explored by Christian psychologists, counsellors and theologians. The theological arguments have been explored in Chapter 1 (see 'Image as Relational'). The following section will explore the development within modern psychology of an attachment emphasis, as this gives contemporary secular value to this core principle within the Waverley Model and provides an overarching framework through which abnormality may be viewed.

Freud and biological drives

Freud emphasised bodily drives as the foundational 'thirsts' of the human personality, although he recognised that somatic drives such as sex, would impact our minds as well, and so became central to explaining human motivation and psychopathology. For Freud therefore, physical drives (the id) are primary in contrast to the Waverley Model which posits spiritual (relational) drives as foundational. Freud states: 'the power of the id expresses the true purpose of the individual organism's life. This consists in the satisfaction of its innate needs.'[158]

Crabb further illuminates the distinction between Freud and the Waverley Model on the issue of what constitutes our primary drive by first discussing the parallel between the position of Freud and his own model (very similar to Hughes'). Both agree that individuals are naturally motivated to meet their own desires; however, the resolution as to how to fulfil these desires is contrasted: for Freud a weakening of the conscience (superego) within reality and social acceptability is promoted; whereas for Crabb, allowing a God-centred conscience to flourish promotes Christ-likeness – the goal of healthy personality. With regard to the primacy of biological drives, Freud's model does not require an innate connection to the environment; rather, this happens only pragmatically as a means of regulating biological satisfaction and frustration – 'it is possible and even necessary to speak of a person divorced from his interpersonal context'.[159] It seems clear that an essential divide underpins such contrasts – Freud's view may be identified with modernity's individualism. Here personhood is primarily defined in reference to self rather than others; whereas Hughes' and Crabb's views in this regard may be aligned with much contemporary theological anthropological formulations which embrace the environment (relationships) and our connection to it as a primary motivator in self-development and identity formation.

Fairbairn and relationships

Other psychoanalysts during Freud's lifetime and in the decades after his death challenged his model of motivation by emphasising relationships as a primary issue. One such school of thought – object relations theory – focuses upon the importance of internal representations (objects) of interpersonal relationships, eg mother. Whilst different theorists within this school use important terms to mean different things, and sometimes conflict in their views, they hold in common an opposition to Freud's belief that biological drives are primary explanatory mechanisms for understanding emotional and behavioural problems. Alternatively, they all accept the desire to connect to another person as primary.[160] Fairbairn, an early Object Relations Theorist, put it as follows: 'libidinal attitudes are relatively unimportant in comparison with object relationships... the object and not the gratification is the ultimate aim of libidinal striving.'[161] Such a polemical choice – the primacy of relationships or biology – can be challenged by a view of personhood which is essentially 'relational substance', (see Chapter 1 – Vitz's definition) where both biological and relational drives are equally primordial, and where satisfaction of one element is founded upon the other, not in opposition to it. As Looker points out, 'bodily urges and attachment needs are intimately connected'.[162] In polemical terms, Fairbairn critiques Freud:

> *Freud's libido theory has remained one of the cornerstones in the edifice of psycho-analytical thought... in my opinion it is high time that the attention of the psychopathologist, which in the past has been successively focused, first upon impulse, and later upon the ego, should now be focused upon the object towards which the impulse is directed.*[163]

For Fairbairn, it was the loss of or failure to obtain intimacy with another which evoked 'splitting' in the ego and the formation of multiple part objects which fragment the self, and which are the developmental roots of psychopathology. Fairbairn was equally critical of Freud's theory of development through psycho-sexual stages. Alternatively, he proposed that we develop through various stages of relational dependence. He also proposed that it was our perception of caregivers that comprised our psychological development and formed our internal structures. This stance is echoed by Hughes' idea that self-worth is largely a derivative of our appraisal of the messages we internalise from others, especially those from our parents. Criticisms have been levelled at the extent to which infants in their early years have the cognitive capacities to 'interpret' their experiences. Stern offers a useful outline of several developmental 'schemas' of earlier infant capacities. Beyond the general mechanisms of internalisation and interpretation, Hughes does not offer a detailed account of the processes leading to an emerging sense of self; rather he focuses upon a consequence of it – our self-worth. Such an emphasis has value in keeping as 'centre stage' a self that is morally responsible, ie now that I am a 'self', what kind of 'self' am I? – good or bad, reflecting God as righteous and so imagining Him or conversely perverting this image.

In summary, Fairbairn believed abnormal development arose out of the failure to achieve a mature dependence on 'the other'. This emphasis clearly parallels the core principles of the Waverley Model, albeit that the latter works out this principle ultimately in a relationship with God through Christ (in its most explicit form) and so also with other human beings who may meet relational needs to some extent. The partial ability of temporal objects to satisfy our relational 'thirst' (drives), always leaves the necessity of finding a God relationship, as only here can the necessary resources for satisfaction be permanently found; all other objects of love, being by their 'creatureliness' and 'createdness' both temporary and themselves needy and incomplete, will not suffice, but disappoint (end up as 'broken cisterns'), if we look to them for ultimate satisfaction.

Bowlby – relationships and biology

The inclusion of embodied personhood within the Waverley Model is in contrast to that of Crabb (see Chapter 1) and is helpful with regards to a concept of human relations that embraces biological factors. This connection is a significant concept for attachment theory which grew out of object relations theory. As attachment theory also emphasises the quality of relationships as determinant of health or pathology, a brief outline of its features will follow.

John Bowlby (1907–1990) was the founder of attachment theory, and proposed that the quality of the relationship between a child and its mother or primary caregiver was a crucial feature in developing mental health or pathology. Bowlby stressed the importance of a child's proximity to its mother as this had survival advantages in personal and evolutionary terms. For Bowlby, the survival of an individual's genes is the ultimate goal and this is a key difference as compared to Fairbairn. Like Fairbairn, Bowlby believed that the need to relate was not a by-product of a more fundamental instinct – children are believed to attach even if caregivers do not meet their biological needs. On a cognitive level, Bowlby departed from Freud's topographical model and developed a concept termed 'internal working models' in which he developed the work of Piaget and Clark on information processing. Bowlby asserted that the organisation of attachment behaviours such as crying, smiling and following were mediated by cognitive factors; where the child's inner world (symbolic representations of important others: mother, father; self, world) was developed and acted upon. Bowlby's 'internal working model' corresponds to Fairbairn's use of 'object relations' but emphasises an individual's construction of their perceptions of good and bad objects. These conclusions about the world shape future expectations, which in turn provide the foundation for developing plans of action.

A child's ability to locate its attachment figure and how that figure responds to the child is a key facet of the child's 'working model of the world'.[164] In the Waverley Model this correlates to the development of security or insecurity depending on the quality of attachment. In a working model of the self, a key theme is how acceptable or unacceptable the child is as construed via evaluations of the attachment figure. Out of this a sense of self-worth is believed to develop – Hughes' second necessity of human identity. Low self-esteem will be derived from the perception that a caregiver regards the child as unacceptable; high self-esteem if the child's perception is that the caregiver is generally accepting. In general terms, these working models persist over time, and where they are detrimental to a constructive dependence, form the basis of pathological views of the self and others; this becomes the arena in which healing needs to occur. In the positive case, which for Bowlby includes parents who can be sensitive to, and respond to a child's attachment needs, a healthy, secure sense of self will emerge, whose working model of self includes appropriate self-help abilities, but also the idea that they are 'worthy of help should difficulties arise'.[165] In the converse case, Bowlby asserts that an insecure attachment creates a personality rooted in anxiety, over-dependence and immaturity, which he claims studies show make up the bulk of psychiatric populations. Furthermore, Bowlby believed that verbal and non-verbal communication were the means by which working models were generated, maintained and transmitted to the next generation. This aspect of Bowlby's theory provides a theoretical backdrop to the process of change evidenced in psychotherapy – a talking cure amidst an empathic, sensitive relationship. This issue will be expanded upon in the next chapter ('Model of Psychotherapy').

Accounts of health and pathology which are centred around the issue of needy dependence on 'the other', such as those of Bowlby and Fairbairn, resonate well with an approach like the Waverley Model. It proposes that a mature dependence is a virtue, not a sign of immaturity as in the autonomous self of hyper-modernity. In addition, the concept that we internalise our relationships, ie that external experiences become part of our inner world, corresponds with biblical ideas of marriage (two become one); the body of Christ (1 Cor. 12), and that God in-dwells us.

I have sought to affirm the value of a relational emphasis within modern psychological theories, especially via object relations and attachment theory as they began to deviate from Freud's focus on biological drives. I have argued, however, that all three approaches can be complementary regarding explanations of motivation, rather than in opposition to each other. These theories give contemporary psychological credence to the relational emphasis of the traditional Waverley Model and are made more explicit in the adaptations of it for which this book argues. I have also outlined that from a biblical world-view, all three secular theories (even when regarded as complementing each other to form a broader notion of motivation) are limited by concepts that omit the benefit provided by a God relationship. This latter focus is distinctive of the Waverley Model in articulating the necessary specific 'object' (God) of mature dependency which thus defines ultimate health and pathology; normality and abnormality.

Abnormality and neuroscience

In recent years neuroscientific research has added objective weight to the idea that relationality needs to be understood in embodied terms.

Over the past thirty years, technological advances have made it possible to observe brain maturation via the use of Magnetic Resonance Imaging (MRI). In general, findings show that the brain develops over the whole life span, but that these developments over the first few years are especially important for shaping patterns of relating both in the present and the future. This is because the developing organisation of the brain is a function of both genetic and environmental factors. According to Schore, seventy percent of the structure of the social/emotional part of the human brain is added after birth and is adaptive to early experience. Schore outlines how the social/emotional brain (prefrontal cortex) in particular develops over the first eighteen months in response to our attachment environment. Gerhardt, in relation to emotional regulation (a key issue in pathology), concludes that the scientific evidence shows that babyhood is a crucial time. This is because several systems that manage emotion (stress response, responsiveness of neurotransmitters and neural pathways which encode our assumptions as to how close relationships work) are not fully present at birth. Schore describes the process of neural connection, which is crucial to learning as a 'use it or lose it' mechanism. This is evidenced starkly by research carried out on Romanian orphans. Left in their cots all day due to lack of available carers, and thereby deprived of significant relational connection, these children 'had virtual black holes where their orbito frontal cortex should be'.[166] In short, our brains develop in part as a 'mirror' of our earliest and most significant carers, and that this 'plasticity' has a survival function. Where this environment is intrinsically hostile, either by direct abuse ('sins of commission') or neglect ('sins of omission'), the experience is embodied, encoded in orbito cortical structures which become our temperamental self – deeply set patterns of mistrust, alarm, hyper-arousal etc which form the basis of later pathological patterns if not corrected.

How is correction possible if these patterns are rooted in brain structures? The possibility of correction is biblically founded upon the vocation given to humanity in the creation account of Genesis. Green defines it as:

individuality within community and the human capacity for
self-transcendence and morality – that is, the capacity to make
decisions on the basis of self-deliberation, planning and action
on the basis of that decision, and responsibility for these decisions
and actions.[167]

As Green notes, the concrete outworking of the creation call to be different (holy), when compared to other creatures (animals), finds expression elsewhere in Scripture covering varied aspects of life that may impact upon our mental wellbeing. For example, Leviticus 19 – family and community respect (vv3,32); religious loyalty (vv4–8,25–31); economic relationships (vv9–10); workers' rights (v13); social compassion (v14); judicial integrity (v15); neighbourly attitudes and conduct (vv16–18); distinctiveness (v19); sexual integrity (vv20–22); exclusion of idols and the occult (vv26–31); racial equality (vv33–34); and commercial honesty (vv35–36). Hope of transformation beyond historically shaped pathological patterns is, as Brueggemann asserts, ultimately rooted in God's holiness. The possibility exists of not being confined by our history but shaped by the hope of 'end times' fullness – restoration of His holy image with which we were originally created.

It can be seen therefore that in aligning our relational patterns to God's created design (imaging God), we become truly human. In addition, the adapted Waverley Model proposed in this book visually portrays the connection between the external world and our core identity (spiritual area). Furthermore, this identity cannot be separated from our body which may have been impaired due to the impact of non-optimal relational conditions earlier in our development. However, despite these limitations, the Bible offers hope that amidst a God relationship we are still able to transcend such limitations and image God as holy – what Green calls our 'unassailable vocation'.

Given the evidence outlined in this chapter, it would be expected that in any individual case of abnormality, causal explanations could relate to any or all of the following domains – physical, psychological, social, environmental and spiritual. Consequently, a method of counselling would need to be one capable of responding constructively to this broad conception of factors. This method will be explored in the next chapter, 'Model of Psychotherapy'.

Abnormality – individual agency and context

The following section aims to locate the importance of relationality amidst our biological and volitional capacities. This preserves a space for explanations in which individual freedom operates within the broader network of relationships; these in turn provide boundaries within around which willing may occur.

One danger of basing a model of abnormality upon ideas regarding relational deficits alone is that it leaves little room for personal responsibility in relation to pathological outcomes. It fosters a view of pure victimhood and the logical consequence of blaming the parents (or some other external factor), for our problems. Alternatively, a model of sin that has been articulated in Chapter 1, including 'original sin' as opposed to McFadyen's 'originating in sinful relationships', holds a balance regarding pathology as both personal and systemic in origin, internal and external in causation, and multi-factorial, rather than reducing it to one issue. This in turn preserves a space for human agency and individual accountability for pathology (unless it is deemed to be purely genetic) which ironically is the basis of hope: we can act not just react, and so may choose reparation towards more healthy patterns of relating. It has been noted by Johnson and Jones that the concept of the will and resultant agency has been marginalised by a psychological tradition rooted in an empirical theory of knowledge. Furthermore, within the context of counselling, approaches lacking a significant concept of human agency will struggle to embrace the core therapeutic ethic of autonomy. Johnson is most helpful in offering a nuanced account of agency which preserves human responsibility in choosing, yet gives weight to numerous factors which influence and thus contextualise our decisions and actions. This kind of explanation flows from the more 'open-ended' dialogical portrayal of personhood for which this book is arguing. Johnson's account includes six contextual factors.

They are:

1. *Biology* – genetic, hormonal, morphological;

2. Identity – life choices only make sense in the light of who we are – in Waverley terms this links the volitional area to the spiritual, and is but one example of why the model needs to be drawn as open ended with perforated circles – indicating dynamic intra-relatedness of the 'five areas of functioning', always operating amidst the 'outside world' (my extra 'category');

3. *Narrative* – our identity unfolds through the history of our relatedness – a developmental pathway 'journey'. Johnson puts it as follows:

> *We act according to purposes, goals developed and shaped in the past and related to the persons and events that are a part of our story. Our actions express a pilgrimage from our earliest years to the celestial or infernal city. Without a history there is no agency.*[168]

4. *Environment* – includes both physical and social. Any specific environment will open up and close down 'action opportunities'. Because such contexts are key to our core identity, these bodily or external conditions form part of our internal world. Socially sensitive choosing would be derived in part by these conditions;

5. *Goods* – we are set in cultures which communicate values by asserting what goods are desirable. As has been noted previously (Chapter 2, 'Model of Personality') a cornerstone of the Waverley Model's notion of motivation is desire (thirst, longing), which may be focused on 'greater' or 'lesser goods' which yield more or less pathological outcomes. As a result of the above, in Johnson's case study, set in contemporary USA, a Ferrari not a Raleigh Runabout would generally be desired;

6. *Linguistic/*Rational*e* – continually repeated cultural stories strengthen values via things said and thought and portray good or bad consequences from actions (vicarious reinforcement).

It is arguable as to whether some of Johnson's six categories are separable. 'Identity', 'narrative', 'goods', and 'linguistic/rationale' all appear as aspects of cultural conditions, especially if identity is worked out with relational aspects, although not exclusively so. There appear to be no objective criteria for establishing how to categorise elements of our external world. Any division, including Johnson's, seems somewhat arbitrary – semantic and pragmatic. In my amended model I have sought to avoid these issues by utilising one all-embracing category 'outside world' (see Appendix B). Being deliberately non-specific, this denotation can be 'filled out' according to relevant conditions for each individual, for example; in certain cases, church will be a highly significant element, whereas for others it will be irrelevant.

Johnson's account of limited freedom arises as one possible perspective amidst a long standing broader philosophical debate around human freedom and determinism. This has been touched upon in Chapter 1 regarding concepts of imago Dei and sin. In this section a more limited point is intended regarding the development of abnormality which is not proven to be reducible to one cause – individual choices or environmental conditions.

Retaining a balance between individual and systemic causes of abnormality enables a multidimensional account of abnormality (as above), beyond a purely biological (illness) or purely relational (historical reaction/defence). Along with human agency and willing, relational deprivation as an explanatory mechanism of abnormality becomes a predictor not a determinant. Thus it could be said, and attachment research findings support this, that upon eliciting a description of an individual's early relational environment, it could be presumed more or less probable that abnormal behaviour would result. Jones and Butman sum up this issue as follows:

> *We are certainly influenced in powerful and significant ways by past relationships. We do not have to assume, however, that this history 'forces' us to behave in a predetermined way, but rather provides 'probabilities' of how we will act.*[169]

The nature of the relationship is not so much akin to a scientific, inexorable, universal law but more like proverbial wisdom – if 'x' then probably 'y'. In this light, we may interpret correctly 'cause' and 'effect' statements within the book of Proverbs, eg 22:6 ('Start children off on the way they should go, and even when they are old they will not turn from it'). The proverbial language may sound literally absolute in its prediction, but this is for the sake of simplicity of thought, not an absolute description of all truth relating to these two phenomena.

Summary and evaluation

In all of this, we may conclude that the general emphasis given to the importance of early styles of relationship in personality development makes sense, especially if we hold a model of imago Dei that is relational. It may be expected that relatively healthy people would emerge from relational patterns that reflect God's relational character; and conversely, that relatively abnormal people would emerge from relational patterns that do not reflect God's character. Jones and Butman rightly assert that our most profound relationships (with parents, grandparents etc) will deeply shape our personalities: that deprived parents may in turn deprive their children – this is one approach to interpreting Exodus 34:7 ('he punishes the children and their children for the sin of parents to the third and fourth generation'). Designed to fully function in a God relationship, we will not find all the resources necessary to build a mature self, as biblically defined, amidst broken and finite relationships.

In explaining individual abnormality, a balanced biblical perspective should at least take into consideration the following: location, culture, history, parents, genetic make-up; all of these operating alongside an individual's particular choices. Thus, an individual who is considered to be making healthy choices (aligning the self with Christ's pattern) may still suffer 'mental ill-health' as a result of the destructive effects of the other factors which comprise a rounded perspective on what contributes to human wellbeing. Conversely, an individual who has benefited from favourable contingent factors such as good parenting, genetics and cultural values may still make subsequent choices which undermine relatively healthy foundations and so produce pathological outcomes. Neither personal choice, nor 'unchosen' contingencies fully determine either normality or abnormality.

As Palmer puts it, 'a human being is whole – a bio-psycho-social unity'.[170] In any individual case of abnormality, explanations of causal factors could relate to any or all of these domains. Consequently, a method of psychotherapy would need to be one capable of responding constructively to this broad conception of factors. This method will now be explored in the following chapter, 'Model of Psychotherapy'.

Chapter 5

Model of Psychotherapy

This chapter will explore the Waverley Model's theory of psychotherapy. Rather than drawing distinctions between these terms, 'psychotherapy' and 'counselling' will be used interchangeably. In this context 'model of psychotherapy' refers to the therapeutic process. Focus is especially upon what elements are necessary in order to foster positive change (which we'll examine in the first three sections of this chapter) and how the Holy Spirit's involvement may be understood (which we'll explore in next two sections). Additionally, it will be discussed as to how Christian counselling, if rooted in a wisdom Christology approach, will at times agree with and at others differ from secular approaches (see the last three sections of this chapter).

These issues emerge from the ideas set forth in the previous chapters, as an approach to treating problems needs to cohere with particular assumptions inherent within its personality theory and which sets the frame of reference for the conception and articulation of a problem.

Assessment and diagnosis

From the perspective of the Waverley Model, the counselling process is divided into three phases – exploration, diagnosis and resolution. This is defended on the grounds that 'most agree with this strategy' despite many different approaches being available to accomplish it. However, some maintain this is an overstatement: an approach which includes an 'assessment' or 'diagnosis' is antithetical to more humanistically oriented traditions of therapy. Not only is diagnosis regarded as unwarranted but also as actively detrimental to client wellbeing. Rogers believed that the agents of positive change reside largely within an individual and would emerge when pain is reduced, not when an 'accurate diagnosis' is offered. Joyce and Sills acknowledge the unhelpful nature of adopting an 'objective' expert stance in formal diagnosis – it implies people are fixed/static; it can depersonalise the uniqueness of a client; it can make the therapist appear superior and so can foster undue reliance on 'the expert'. However, they also assert that, 'We are always assessing ('diagnosing') in so far as that all humans are meaning-makers. Our way of making sense of the world can be said to be an ongoing form of assessment or diagnosis.'[171] This perspective views diagnosis as a continuous facet of relating in counselling (and life in general) and not a formal procedure to be carried out at a particular point or stage in the process. Other major therapeutic traditions wholeheartedly embrace diagnosis as a distinct and positive procedure. Beck, the founder of cognitive therapy, regards it as essential unless a previous diagnosis has already been carried out. Contemporary cognitive theorists also share the same view. More generally, Neenan and Palmer assert that any problem-solving psycho-educational approach to helping people is likely to endorse 'diagnosis' (although other similar descriptive terms may be used, like case conceptualisation, formulation, definition of the problem) as a specific procedure related to a 'stage' in their work with clients. From a Christian perspective, Shields and Bredfelt's helping model, which they claim can be used broadly by pastors, Christian laypersons, teachers, those involved in discipleship and those who want to help a friend, also takes diagnosis (the word they use is 'problem definition') as a set phase of the counselling process.

Whatever differing philosophical position or method of assessing/diagnosing we adopt, Palmer and McMahon's argument regarding its pragmatic necessity is persuasive, rooted in the possibility that non-assessment could lead to the use of an approach that research shows has no value in helping a client's specific problem. It is reasonable to assume that in therapy both parties implicitly suppose that the therapist has some relevant skills and/or insights (expertise) that make sense of why both agree to work together, as opposed to a client turning to any other person for help. Regarding clients, Joyce and Sills state, 'They came with the reasonable expectation that the counsellor has the expertise to help with the problem in as short a time as possible.'[172] From a therapist's perspective, there needs to be some rational justification for agreeing to work with specific clients (and their issues) in order to be operating within professional ethical boundaries which require both beneficence and non-maleficence.

It would appear that some form of diagnosis is inevitable, whether formal or informal, explicit or implicit, or as part of a 'stage'/'phase' or as an ongoing aspect of relating. Having said this, it is quite clear that on the basis of Waverley Model Trainers' Notes, their method sits clearly within the problem-solving oriented approaches, along with its subsequent benefits and potential problems. The problems, as noted above, may arise, not because of diagnosis as a principle or concept, but as a consequence of the way in which it is brought into operation, which may greatly vary. In the Waverley Model, diagnosis (phase two) proceeds towards and is the basis for resolution (phase three). The way in which phase three is defined adds gravitas to the Waverley Model's 'diagnosis' as implying an educational process directed by an expert – the counsellor. Within the overview of the three-phase counselling process, phase three is articulated as follows: 'This is the stage where the counselee is presented with the biblical solutions to his/her problem.'[173] This description regarding the objective of phase three might be construed firstly on theological grounds, as evidenced by Hughes' evangelical commitment stated in the CWR mission statement: 'Applying God's Word to everyday life and relationships.' Secondly, the objective of phase three may be understood on personal grounds, given Hughes' journey from evangelist to counsellor – Christian counselling as 'problem-based evangelism'. Additionally, the language of 'presentation' to describe the method of applying the diagnosis and 'interview' as a synonym for a counselling session fits well with modernity – the philosophical backdrop of Hughes' formative years. Having said this, Hughes himself referred to his model as 'a framework not a straightjacket'. This sentiment and the adjustment of language within the Waverley literature allows students space to integrate the basic principles of the framework into an individual style. This can be both sensitive to context and the preferences of therapist and client, for instance greater or lesser desire for an ordered, 'step by step' process.

This space for individualising the process appears to be important: Cummings and Lucchese's research acknowledges that alongside our core values influencing the adoption of specific approaches, incidental issues also play a part, possibly even a primary role. These individual factors include the supervisor's orientation and that of their personal therapist, plus social, cultural, personal and historical events, all of which may be in conflict with the therapist's core personality preference. A personalised approach helps minimise this possible dissonance. A static relationship between practitioner and orientation is also doubtful, and so room for 'evolution' needs to exist.

This current work is itself an attempt to argue for 'evolution' not 'revolution', by setting forth the strengths of the Waverley Model alongside contemporary theological developments regarding, for instance, imago Dei. Additionally, scientific research on human functioning, for instance neuroscience and that which is directly related to the therapeutic process, has also been utilised for the same purpose.

The focus of change

This section will demonstrate how the Waverley Model and relevant teaching material has been adapted increasingly to emphasise relationality as a key aspect of therapeutic change. 'Change' in this context parallels 'Resolution', ie phase three of Hughes' Model.

As discussed in Chapter 3, 'Model of Health', the Waverley Model articulates movement towards health primarily in terms of the process of repentance. The concept of repentance is articulated in specific terms relating to Christ-dependence: 'our crucial needs or deep longings can only be met in a deep and ongoing relationship with Christ.'[174] Beyond this, the effects of our social context are also acknowledged as impacting healthy development, but only secondarily: 'Other people may support us, strengthen us and minister to our needs but we are complete only in Him.'[175]

Given the emphasis on Christ-dependence for health, pathology is closely linked to God-displacement and is regarded as the core dynamic of sin: 'The essence of sin is God-displacement. We expel God from the place which He has reserved for Himself – the centre of our beings.'[176] As a result of the above theological emphases, Hughes regards the counsellor's task as primarily helping the client become aware of how misplaced dependency is related to and maintains problems, and so blocks the change necessary for promoting health.

For Hughes, this 'core' spiritual repentance precedes and is the motive for potential change in the other four areas which make up the structure of his model of personality. For example, aligning our thinking with a biblical perspective of the self, others and the world (Rational Area); changing goals and related behaviours (Volitional Area); managing emotions (Emotional Area) and looking after our bodies (Physical Area). Additionally, Hughes warns that changes in the latter four areas of personality, if not predicated upon his notion of a spiritual repentance, will only lead to self-sufficiency – the very issue that Hughes asserts is at the centre of most of our problems. Historically the Waverley literature has encompassed awareness of how relational factors such as transference and counter-transference can mediate the process of therapeutic change. In the past this has not been a significant emphasis, perhaps due to Hughes' desire to keep explicitly scriptural principles as a central foundation for change. However, relational factors as an aspect of potential healing are increasingly emphasised in response to empirically based outcome research in psychotherapy.

It should be noted that many Christian counselling approaches have always emphasised the central importance of the therapeutic relationship as being a key agent of positive change. Hurding cites those embracing evangelical, liberal and Catholic traditions. Hughes, whilst focusing upon the power of Scripture, shows an understanding that a 'turn to the word' must not be undertaken outside of relational sensitivity and a compassionate presence with the client. He states:

> *the biggest single mistake that people make when trying to help someone... is to turn too quickly to the Scriptures... If there is one thing I have learned over 50 years of helping people with their problems, it is that people in difficulty don't care how much you know until they know how much you care.*[177]

These concerns of Hughes help avoid a stereotypical view of the Waverley Model as promoting Scripture as a 'prescriptive pill to cure all ills'. Indeed, the quotations of both Hughes and Crabb cited at the beginning of this book demonstrate an openness on both parts to develop their respective models in the light of new data as part of an always incomplete 'journey of discovery'. This 'journey' implies potential modification and adaptation, which is evidenced, for example, by a comparison of Waverley's counselling curriculum for the Certificate of Christian Counselling 2000–2001 and 2010–2011. Various additions have been made to the latter (absent in the former) which place a greater emphasis on the relevance of our relationality in fostering therapeutic change:

1. The 'five areas of functioning' of the traditional Waverley Model are now preceded by a 'relational area'. This area highlights the importance of an emphasis upon the value of the therapeutic relationship.

2. The counselling skills module now starts with a lecture on the therapeutic relationship. This primary place in the order of subjects taught is intentional, as all other skills are regarded as either adding to, or undermining this important phenomenon.

3. 'Process Groups' now occur weekly throughout the certificate course, and regularly in each of the other two years of the degree. They are also a regular feature on the degree course held at Waverley Abbey House. These groups express the value Waverley now places on students' relational awareness developing through an ongoing experience of 'encounter', and reflection on this experience.

These three adaptations are examples of a changing emphasis which impacts all three modules constituting the certificate course: theory, skills and personal/professional development. In addition to the above, a recently published Waverley counselling course reader written by Kallmier, who was until 2010 CWR's Director of Training, devotes one chapter to the therapeutic relationship, placing a high value upon it. He states:

The counsellor's knowledge, skills, experience... are some of the important factors in a successful counselling association. But these are not critical or influential factors. The most significant ingredient in successful counselling is the nature and quality of the relationship between the client and the counsellor.[178]

Methods of change

In this brief section, it will be argued that a variety of interventions are necessary in order to offer optimum conditions for the promotion of therapeutic change. This variety is coherent with biblical imperatives used for helping people.

Within the context of relatedness, the Waverley Model gives space for a variety of interventions that may be utilised with any given client, at any given time, amidst the unfolding counselling process. This freedom arises from regarding the Waverley Model as a framework of principles to be creatively applied according to context, personality preference etc, rather than as a 'straightjacket' within which an extensive number of procedures are prescriptively offered. It is in this creative space that the Waverley Model is most obviously practised as an 'art' not as 'science'. Thus, procedurally, wisdom, discernment and judgment are necessary, which from a Christian perspective require a therapist to 'listen to the Spirit of wisdom – the Holy Spirit'. An ongoing dependence on God is therefore necessary, a principle which lies at the heart of Hughes' model of health, not only for the client, but also for therapeutic judgment by the counsellor. This kind of creative discernment is warranted by Scripture itself. In 1 Thessalonians 5:14, Paul advocates a variety of interventions to aid 'people helping': 'And we urge you, brothers and sisters, warn those who are idle and disruptive, encourage the disheartened, help the weak, be patient with everyone.' Elsewhere in Scripture other forms of responses are encouraged including loving (Matt. 22:39; John 15:12), comforting (2 Cor. 1:4; 2:7) and grieving (James 4:9). Jones and Butman sum up the point well: 'clearly what is needed is a flexible repertoire of approaches, grounded in coherent theory and deeply respectful of the complexity and profundity of human struggles.'[179] Regarding the

Waverley Model, the above principle can potentially be applied when working in any of the five areas of functioning, thereby providing a flexibly creative ethos through which the goals of phase three (resolution) may be attained.

The Holy Spirit and change

In the introductory chapter to this book, it was stated that a Christian model of counselling must address the issue of the process of change in relation to the activity of the Holy Spirit. Is the Spirit inevitably involved in transformation toward health? If this is so, is the role explicit or implicit? If explicit, what form might this take regarding processes and/or techniques and interventions? In answering these questions, general conceptions regarding the Holy Spirit (top level) will be followed by an attempt to seek their application to the counselling process (bottom level). The focus will centre upon the 'work', not the 'person' of the Holy Spirit.

Williams states the issue of the identification of the Spirit's work as one of revelation: 'how is God heard or seen to be present to the human world?'[180] In its broadest biblical conception, the Holy Spirit sustains all life: 'the breath of life' (Gen. 6:17). In the Old Testament context of creation, the Spirit connotes all life as a gift from God, and thus can be given or removed according to God's will. From this perspective, the Spirit is implicit in the existence of all life, ie the Spirit is essential to life everywhere, including a therapeutic encounter in all its nuances. This principle of life being a gift from God and therefore everything which is alive being God-dependent not only relates to the creation narratives, but is echoed throughout the whole of Scripture with non-life (death) beyond the 'edge' of the Spirit. The psalmist therefore fears God taking the Spirit away from him (Psa. 51:11); Job grasps the fact that: 'In his hand is the life of every creature and the breath of all mankind' (Job 12:10).

In relation to human beings in particular, Yong makes the helpful connection between a 'foundational pneumatology' (the Spirit's presence and activity everywhere in the world – including natural, cultural, social, institutional and interpersonal dimensions) and imago Dei in so far as human beings were created uniquely by the divine breath of God. Yong cites both structural and relational aspects of humanity when outworking this distinctiveness – such as rational, volitional, moral and interpersonal. The connection between creation and imago Dei helps move us from a perspective of 'being alive' in general, towards specific qualities which constitute aspects of this human 'life', ie 'to choose freely, to act morally, to relate to others intentionally, to experience interpersonal subjectivity – these are the pneumatological features of human living in the world'.[181] Bearing in mind these features, connections to therapy can be made, such that potentially it becomes a Spirit-infused endeavour, depending upon which goals are being pursued with what methods.

Williams further helps discernment with regard to identifying the Spirit's activity via the delineation of two spheres of operation – the 'charisms' (extraordinary and intermittent) and the characteristic 'fruits' ('ordinary' and more permanent). The distinction can also be stated as the difference between 'gifts' of the Spirit, as opposed to 'life' in the Spirit. The latter is evidenced by moral and relational qualities (for example, Gal. 5:22–23). These qualities will be distinctively Christlike in character, as from a Trinitarian perspective, the Spirit works in conjunction with the Son and proceeds from Him (filioque). This provides grounds from which we may demarcate what endeavours or phenomena belong to the Spirit, as opposed to 'other spirits'. Williams cites the fostering of freedom and maturity (now given Christological shape) as two examples of the Spirit's work. Olthuis gives more detail as to what maturity from a Christian perspective would look like – increased intimacy amidst the relationship of self, others, the earth and God. He states:

> *A healthy person (mature) is neither a separated self in grand isolation nor a fused self without boundaries; rather, he or she is a cohesive, bounded self in wholesome connections, interdependent with other selves, the earth and God.*[182]

Whether we adopt the models of Williams, Olthuis, Crabb, Hughes or others, the significant issue at stake is grasping how each model attempts to unpack a concept of 'full life' as identifiable with the Spirit. Each model may have its own specific focus (although there is significant overlap between them) but each attempts to make phenomenal (ie concrete) that which coheres with 'the life of the Spirit', and hence clarify the type of goals which are worth pursuing and towards which priority may be given.

From a counselling context, successes in liberating a client from the slavish grip of addictions, or in general terms, bringing peace and reconciliation in a marriage relationship, can be identified with the work of the Holy Spirit. Therefore, God's truths can permeate the sphere of counselling by degrees at any given time as goals and methods are utilised which are in consort with the Spirit, albeit not necessarily pursued consciously by the counsellor or client with this aim in mind. Whilst such values and practices as freedom (mastery) and maturity (as exemplified by fruits of the Spirit) are not salvific and hence will not of themselves yield eternal benefits, they will (albeit only temporally) contribute to personal transformations that display Christ-likeness. They will then also in principle conform to a model of health that is ethically consistent with a Christian world-view. Similarly, a therapeutic process which implicitly or explicitly assumes human responsibility, holism and transcendence (if believed to be aspects of a Christian anthropology) may be considered to be conforming to Spirit-enlightened truth. Whilst such philosophical or ethical values are often connected with theism, Slife, Stevenson and Wendt correctly point out that an active God is not necessary when explaining or understanding them. Likewise, specific activities such as praying, meditating, forgiving or being 'mindful' may be understood from either an atheistic or theistic point of view. Whilst there is a conceptual and historical correlation with theism, Taylor points out that they are not uniquely theistic. Similarly, prayer to God can be regarded from a naturalistic perspective as an activity arising out of the projection of human wishes and aspirations. Quite clearly 'spiritual' activities may arise from a human desire to promote self-transcendence and yet unless indwelt by the Holy Spirit as opposed to 'other spirits', will always lead to the diminution of self-hood of which Christ is the criterion of fullness. Williams well captures the balance between a broad life-giving Spirit which manifests freely in diverse and unexpected ways, and yet points Christ-wards. He states:

> *The Son is manifest in a single, paradigmatic figure, the Spirit is manifest in the 'translatability' of that into the contingent diversity of history. Freedom in the Spirit is uncircumscribed; and yet it always has the shape of Jesus the Son[183]*

Having earlier introduced a biblical conception of the cosmic and pervasive activity of the Spirit, it would be consistent to assume the Spirit's presence in the aforementioned activities. However, asserting the Spirit's omnipresence is not tantamount to assuming that the Spirit is therefore the active agent in all endeavours, as the human and demonic spirits must also be accounted for. Slife, Stevenson and Wendt denote a view of pervasive Spirit as 'strong theism' as opposed to 'weak theism', where the activity of the Spirit is presumed to be limited in time (deism) and space (dualism). The amended Waverley Model diagram (see Appendix B) which this book proposes, better portrays the 'strong theism' position through opening up the 'spiritual area' by means of perforating the traditionally closed circles, and showing an open-ended connection with other areas of functioning and the outside world. The latter is left un-delineated precisely to prevent restriction of scope and to avert any temptation towards a dualist interpretation of the Waverley anthropological model.

Wisdom and the Holy Spirit

This section further attempts to link Holy Spirit activity with 'common phenomena' via biblical wisdom. Whilst the moral framework of Old Testament wisdom concurred with covenant law, in general terms, wisdom was a much broader concept. Hilber describes biblical wisdom broadly as both creative and potentially unconventional. He argues reasonably that when referring to counselling interventions and techniques, in order to be deemed 'biblical', they need not be confined to those that are explicit in Scripture.

Crabb has taken a more restrictive view with regards to integrative possibilities: 'Counselling models must demonstrate more than consistency with Scripture, they must in fact emerge from it.'[184] However, the view of biblical wisdom (its nature and function) that has been outlined earlier (Chapter 3) aligns itself with Hilber and thus concurs with his conclusion that the use of Scripture cannot in principle be deemed mandatory in order for an approach to be regarded as 'biblical'. Furthermore, Hilber points out that wisdom, in its broadest biblical sense, is instruction and is often passed down verbally within families (Prov. 4:1). As such it was generally independent of written codes, 'whether covenant law code, canonical wisdom literature itself, or New Testament imperatives'.[185] It follows that a method of evaluating which activities in the counselling process are 'of the Spirit' and hence life-giving and worth pursuing, cannot be reduced to biblical proof text or precedent. Such reduction undermines the ongoing creative aspect of the work of the Spirit as has already been established in this book.

With regard to identifying 'Spirit' activity, Yong's criterion for discernment involves recognition that there is a correlation of logos (word) and pneuma (Spirit) which constitutes all defined things. He states, 'the former being a thing's concrete forms and the latter being the thing's inner habits, tendencies and laws'.[186] Yong argues his case using numerous biblical examples where the activity of the Holy Spirit is distinguished from demonic spirits by reference to their impact upon the phenomenal world, ie concrete appearance or sensory perception. However, Boa argues for caution when using outward phenomena alone to delineate 'spirits', as manifestations can be derived from what he refers to as either 'natural works' or 'spiritual power'. As a result, he helpfully adds, 'true supernatural operations (the work of the Holy Spirit) must be distinguished not by the experiences alone but by the larger context of Christ-centredness and permanent character'.[187]

In light of this, Holy Spirit inspired wisdom would constitute anything which moves clients towards their divinely appointed function and purpose. This is evidenced from a Christological perspective by that which fosters life in all its fullness (John 10:10). The idea of 'fullness' is worked out using shepherd/sheep imagery, in particular the sheep being cared for by the shepherd and thus living contented lives. Kruse renders the existential application as either an enjoyment of a rich life in the here and now, especially if linked with God, or to eternal life after resurrection (John 5:24–29). Kruse deems both possibilities as reasonable of the text. In this context, Beasley-Murray interprets the meaning of 'full life' as the gospel message – eternal life in God's kingdom (inclusive of a current dimension). Elements of this 'fullness', for example high, low or mixed self-esteem (depending on one's doctrinal stance), and their impact upon our humanity, will be interpreted by criteria that constitute doctrines relevant to any specific counselling endeavour. For example, this is why ideas regarding Scripture, sin and imago Dei become pragmatically significant for Christian counsellors and why they occupied a major part of Chapter 1. In order to make clearer the connection between doctrine and counselling goals and related methods, it is helpful to consider in more detail, as a case in point, the contentious issue of human self-regard, often rendered self-esteem. Opposing Christian perspectives and related counselling practices are the outworking of different doctrinal positions relevant to human anthropology. Many engaged in counselling (psychological or pastoral) or theological training will have had to think through this issue.

The nub of the debate is this: in the light of the metanarrative of Scripture (creation, Fall, redemption etc) how should humans think of themselves? There are those who interpret Scripture in a manner that leads to the conclusion that humans should esteem themselves highly because they are made in God's image. One of the major voices in the 1980s 'Self-esteem movement' was Robert Schuller, who declared the values of self-esteem to be the 'new reformation'.[188] Conversely, critical voices such as Adams, Vitz and Bobgan and Bobgan argued their case based on Scripture and regarded self-love as heresy. Commenting on Paul's writings, Adams asserts: 'Nowhere does he say we should feel good about ourselves because we exist, because we were made in the image of God, or even because, in Christ we are made perfect in God's sight.'[189]

Others have adopted a middle ground. McGrath and McGrath, from a perspective of integrating a biblical and psychological approach, argue that Christian confidence (self-esteem in this context) 'rests totally upon the cross of Christ'. However, they agree that some psychotherapeutic approaches can be useful (despite the fact that they do not rest upon biblical assumptions) – their book aims at 'resolving these tensions'.[190] Stott, having noted the two sides of the debate and relevant influential factors supporting the polarised views, tries to avoid a self-regard that is too high or too low, but which represents a 'sober judgment'. For Stott, like McGrath and McGrath, the cross of Christ supplies the answer: 'it calls us both to self-denial and to self-affirmation'.[191] Stott most helpfully eliminates the dilemma of self-love or loathing by pointing out that the self is not one simple entity. Additionally, Stott asserts that, rooted in creation, we may esteem the part of ourselves which images God, but that at the same time, due to the Fall (the image defaced), we are to 'deny, disown and crucify' that part which no longer reflects (images) Christ.

As regards the Waverley Model, it is logical to assume that self-esteem constitutes a key issue. Compared to Crabb, Hughes has explicitly added self-esteem as an additional core spiritual longing, although as has been argued earlier (see Chapter 2, 'Hughes' and Crabb's Relationality'), this difference does not represent as deep a divide as may first appear. Hughes' position sits most easily with that of Stott, as like Stott, Hughes links the value of a high self-esteem to the context of creation and imago Dei. Again, like Stott, he gives weight to the impact of the Fall in deriving a doctrine of depravity (see Chapter 1, 'Depravity') and a turning to the cross of Christ and the power of redemption by which our true image (and esteem) may be restored.

The question posed earlier (how to discern Holy Spirit inspired wisdom) may be answered when the following criteria are fulfilled: any counselling issue, if approached firstly in a way that is methodologically consistent with Christian ethics and secondly is pursued towards specific goals and outcomes which are Christologically consistent, could in principle be regarded as aspects of 'life in the Spirit'. For instance, work on issues such as sexuality, family life, desire for love and belonging could, if the previous criteria are met, constitute such Holy Spirit inspired wisdom. However, given what has been said earlier relating to three distinctive positions relating to self-esteem, it would necessarily follow that the lines between what is considered Christian and anti-Christian and hence 'of the Spirit' or not, will be drawn very differently. The example of self-esteem clearly demonstrates how our basic assumptions (core doctrines) eventually 'trickle down' to concrete practices in counselling, as each therapist attempts to work in ways they believe are consistent with their version of a Christian world-view. Therefore, a Christian counsellor who holds a doctrine of sin which includes original innocence (both corporate and individual) is likely to positively evaluate aspirations and methods like that of Bradshaw. He wants to reconnect clients with their 'inner child', and hence experience a 'homecoming' which is assumed to be healthy. Cooper sums up the position well:

> *In fact, psychological problems [including low self-esteem – my addition] are always related to a distrust in this basic organismic trustworthiness. We need to stay out of nature's way and allow each person to be self-directing. There is no innate selfishness, self-centeredness or inordinate pleasure-seeking. Thus we need to reconnect with the vitalities of this inherent self-actualizing tendency.*[192]

Alternatively, those who assume some form of original sin, and the resultant sleight upon a pure, good, innocent self (and related esteem) would be less likely to regard purely self-directed methods as yielding ultimate health. This is because they would regard our nature itself as more complex and contradictory, rooted in conflict as opposed to instinctive harmony within the self and towards others. Indeed, for Niebuhr, the core of human original sin is pride and its manifestations of many kinds (he offers four) including self-sufficiency and self-glorification. This inherent state of affairs yields inordinate self-love (esteem) which is thus regarded as part of the problem, not the cure.

In any given case, it will be necessary to make judgments regarding whether 'this client' at 'this specific juncture' of their development has an overtly narcissistic self-regard or an undervalued sense of self. The latter may be more likely to occur where there has been significant abuse (sexual, physical or otherwise) through which a 'self as object', or self without value or dignity/respect has been communicated and internalised. Our doctrinal position, whilst offering a general starting point (assumption), needs to be flexible enough (within limits) to capture the particular variances within our common humanity. It will then meet the criterion of comprehensiveness required of any model of practice, as set out previously. With a history of abuse, a person is likely to be less disposed toward Niebuhr's self-glorifying tendency (although this could occur as a defensive 'reaction formation') as compared to an individual whose salient relational history has communicated great value. Thus, some adjustment of our general premises can help avoid an over-generalised rigid method, borne of lack of practical wisdom and discernment. This latter problem has been highlighted by Fouque and Glachan concerning empirical evidence that 'biblical counsellors' were 'too fixed' with their methods towards clients who had been sexually abused.[193] This research further illustrates the value of Hughes' assertion that his model should not be regarded as a 'straightjacket' but as a framework of principles that need to be applied with both discernment and sensitivity.

In light of the issues highlighted here, along with the more extensive discussion of wisdom in Chapter 3 and of Scripture in Chapter 1, I conclude by quoting Hilber. He succinctly sums up the position for which I have argued with regard to discernment of Spirit-imbued wisdom:

> *Scripture guides the appropriation of knowledge from other sources and in counselling, (sic) the value content, theoretical orientation and methods of psychotherapy are ultimately subordinate to biblical theology and ethics.*[194]

Implications for Counselling (a closer look)

With the proviso set out in the previous section, a more detailed discussion of specific counselling goals and interventions will follow. A comparison and contrast between Christian and secular perspectives will be founded upon Dueck's framework, itself developed from Niebuhr's five categories of how the church throughout history has interacted with culture. Focus will be on Dueck's first two categories, 'critique' and 'analogy', as they provide the clearest means by which comparison and contrast can be made. A biblical wisdom approach, because of its creation and anthropocentric focus, gives grounds for engagement with secular practices ('analogy'); however, wisdom's theistic and Christological aspects result in distinctiveness ('critique'). This balance means that a wholesale absorption (syncretism) is avoided; secular insights may be appropriated (Hughes and Crabb's 'Spoiling the Egyptians') where a Christian world-view is not compromised. Hurding, whilst offering an historical overview of the above factors, expresses the value of an approach encompassing both special and general revelation:

> *At best, the people of God have sifted, evaluated and challenged contemporary thinking in the light of Scripture; at worst, they have found the approach of the 'two horizons' too daunting and have either escaped into the bolt-hole of reaction or embraced the cosy anonymity of assimilation, taking in presuppositions and objectives of the surrounding culture with little or no critical reflection.[195]*

The selection of topics covered is necessarily limited, and is intended to illustrate the above rather than offer a comprehensive, systematic coverage. The list extends Irving's previous work on this topic. Given the discussion of wisdom earlier (Chapter 3), the supporting evidence will be predominately confined to secular therapies, specifically psychodynamic, person-centred and cognitive behavioural, as they represent three well established and prevalent modalities.

Analogy

This approach assumes continuity between Christ in the life of the Church and the world. Dueck sums it up well: 'This approach begins with God's self-disclosure and then moves by way of analogy from God's covenant to creation, from God's action to ours, from the Christ event to historical events.'[196]

Whilst there is not an absolute parallel across therapeutic modalities, generally speaking both secular psychotherapy and biblical wisdom assume the following:

a. The value of developing skills which aid successful practical living involving physical, emotional, cognitive, moral and spiritual realms. Some secular approaches explicitly utilise 'skills training' language when describing goals and methods of attaining them.[197] Others dislike the modernist connotations of a skills training approach – control, mastery via an expert – to therapy. However, it could be argued that the values and practices which are adopted by the latter are really a different set of skills under another name; for example, for Olthuis 'a way of being' is clearly the key therapeutic 'skill' which is modelled so that clients likewise may adopt this 'way of being'.[198]

b. The importance of human dignity. Each places a high value on persons as they are regarded as possessing inherent worth and are endowed with attributes and potential which are worth prizing.

c. Personal responsibility for choices and behaviour. In general terms people are regarded as volitional and thus therapists must avoid imposition of their own values and ways of living. This could be identified by the way therapists work with client transference (especially idealised forms). Therapists would thus avoid acting on the 'pull' of a client to become the 'expert with all the answers'.[199] The BACP fosters respect for client autonomy, and hence implicitly supports human agency and volition.

d. The value of reflection on suffering which become the means of growth and adaptation. As discussed in Chapter 3, biblical wisdom can also include direct instruction regarding the passing on of skills and knowledge. This element, according to Hurding's scheme of 'analogy', best fits with cognitive behavioural approaches rather than psychodynamic or person-centred ones.

e. Human flourishing and growth occurs amidst an ongoing process of reflective learning and adaptation. This could be facilitated via person-centred or CBT values and practices.[200]

f. The value of tasks such as making judgments, gaining experience, introspection, gaining knowledge, skills, obtaining insights from mistakes. In CBT for example, behavioural experiments set as homework may confirm new 'balanced thinking', or the converse. In the latter case this provides grounds from which the new 'balanced belief' may be discovered to be inadequate, and hence is further refined.

g. An individual's psychological complexity including unconscious dynamics which require specific skills if they are to be worked through. Psychodynamic therapists give a special focus to this aspect of human functioning, although there is a broad consensus across approaches regarding the relevance of unconscious processes. Forshaw states: 'we think of the wide agreement in psychology that the bulk of the individual's self is held in a mysterious system called the unconscious.'[201] Young, Klosko and Weishaar, from their cognitively-based approach, affirm many parallels (and some differences) with psychodynamic approaches, including working with transference and counter-transference phenomena arising from the unconscious. Rogers, from a person-centred perspective, also accepts as valid the concept of transference phenomena, albeit that he believes acute transference is less prevalent than do psychodynamic therapists. Additionally, the person-centred therapist, whilst accepting the possibility of attribution biases towards them (transference) would expect to resolve them differently – by means of acceptance rather than interpretation, through which the therapist disproves negative unconscious distortions, or overly idealised positive ones. The latter may be achieved by the therapist's self-acceptance as 'less than ideal' and hence the refusal to collude with the client's projection.

h. The necessity of providing a safe space where a non-defensive deep exploration of self can occur – 'to search and be searched'.[202] Safety as a value is most readily identifiable with Rogers' approach as it arises as a corollary to his second core condition for change, namely acceptance. Forshaw, from a contemporary, 'relational' psychodynamic approach, also espouses the virtue of safety (via acceptance and worth) if positive change is to occur. It may be less obvious that cognitive approaches also require relational sensitivity, including a general attitude of acceptance and warmth towards the client. Aron Beck, founder of Cognitive Therapy, gives weight to the necessity of clients being able to 'be themselves' without fear of rejection or judgment from the therapist. According to Beck, this state of affairs is fostered by therapist empathy and concern for the client. Beck argues for the development of cognitive techniques that are founded upon a good therapeutic relationship, constituted by characteristics which parallel Rogers' 'core conditions'. Beck states:

> *The general characteristics of the therapist which facilitate the application of cognitive therapy (as well as other kinds of psychotherapies) include warmth, accurate empathy and genuineness.*[203]

These conditions are regarded as necessary but not sufficient for an optimum therapeutic outcome.

i. Necessity for helpers (in order to be effective), to have personal qualities of self-awareness, genuineness and a positive regard towards those they are trying to help.[204]

Critique

World-views will not only impact therapeutic aims and methods, but also anthropological assumptions. Therefore, in all of these areas, alongside wisdom's anthropocentric focus, room must also be given to the Bible's 'Yahwistic/Christocentric' backdrop which sets the broader interpretive context. Thus, it should not be surprising that a fully integrated Christian psychotherapy should include elements which distinguish it from many popular modern approaches that assume atheism. Dueck sums up the 'critique's' position as a polemic to modern culture (in this context secular therapies): 'Christianity is seen as a way of life entirely separate from the host culture.'[205] It is in this interpretive space that Adams' work makes most sense, although he appears to see little or no room for 'analogy', hence his critique of Hughes' and Crabb's integrative approaches. At the same time, however, it must also be acknowledged that, due to divergent beliefs among Christian counsellors regarding the integration of secular psychology and Christian theology (see in Chapter 1 the 'Summary and Evaluation' of 'Relating Theology and Psychology'), the way in which any one Christian practises therapy will greatly vary from another. 'Critique' shows how a Christian approach will differ from secular approaches in various ways, including the following:

a. 'Fully functioning' persons are always characterised in terms of an active relationship with God which opposes both humanistic and individualistic assumptions. Rogers, on the other hand, articulates 'the good life', or 'fully functioning person' as one who is free to go in any direction, which may or may not include towards God. Similarly, the new mature self of existential psychotherapy is self-referenced. Biblical wisdom, however, determines that a positive response would be given to a client who expresses a desire to explore a relationship with God. Given wisdom's creative emphasis, such a desire could be facilitated by numerous varieties of interventions.

b. The goal of biblical wisdom diverges from that of secular wisdom. The latter includes happiness, integration and self-direction and effective decision making, often interpreted individualistically. However, from a Christian perspective, biblical wisdom seeks 'Christ-following' as primary; happiness (blessing) may emerge as a secondary by-product. This ordering helps limit the potentially destructive corollary which might surface amidst human flourishing and ingenuity – pride and self-determination. Thiselton rightly points out that an unbounded pride of achievement so easily becomes excessive self-veneration to the exclusion of God – the very thing that biblical wisdom seeks to avoid, as the fear of the Lord is regarded as foundational to true wisdom.

c. Biblical wisdom would oppose any approach which assumes or supports racism, sexism, ageism or classism. This arises out of a Christ-centred wisdom interpretive method which bestows a robust value (worth, dignity) upon all humanity.

d. Human responsibility to choose is upheld but an unbridled notion of autonomy or its pursuit as a valued goal would be opposed. Ultimate healthy functioning is conceived as a partnership between God and humanity, where the latter are entrusted to be co-workers with Him restoring creation's intended righteousness. Herein lies a significant tension for Christian counsellors who wish to uphold wisdom's emphasis upon God-dependence amidst a contemporary secular culture. This includes professional bodies which esteem a self-referenced autonomy, such as that outlined in BACP's ethical framework. It could be argued that such compliance to, and fostering of, autonomy may reverse any inclination towards a God-dependence, born of self-poverty, and hence leave clients further removed from a wisdom perspective's view of healthy functioning. Such issues may be resolved in part through consideration of the converse case, where autonomy is actively undermined by evoking a personal crisis rather than, for example, aiding independent problem solving. This state of affairs would be unacceptable, not only because it would undermine other key professional values (for example, 'non-maleficence: a commitment to avoiding harm to the client'[206]), but also undermine a Christian ethic of taking every opportunity to do good to all people at all levels, whether ultimate salvation or on a temporal pragmatic level.

e. Counselling rooted in biblical wisdom would, whenever possible, seek reflection, insight and help beyond the limits of personal experience, and would include revelatory knowledge. This approach arises out of a New Testament perspective which combines wisdom and revelation as embodied in Jesus Christ.

f. The use of Scripture would not be mandatory as a source of helpful knowledge, as biblical wisdom itself points to sources of help beyond the canon of Scripture. However, when Scripture is used, wise judgment would be necessary when deciding which parts of Scripture are relevant at any given point in the counselling process, and in the means of their application.

Summary and evaluation

In this chapter it has been established that when applying the Waverley Model to the therapeutic process, many variations of personal style and practical interventions are possible, and also desirable, in order to avoid an overly rigid application. These principles were founded upon both Scriptural imperatives and empirical research. Within these broad possibilities, limits were defined by reference to means of establishing goals and methods which conform to 'Holy Spirit imbued wisdom'. In particular, Yong's connection between creation and imago Dei was seen to help establish specific attributes (structural and relational) which could be regarded as examples of Christ-likeness, and so would constitute phenomenal 'concrete' expressions of the Holy Spirit's life at work. These phenomena could thus be rendered as products of a Christian counselling approach, even when 'Christ-following' is not pursued consciously. However, positive change could still occur as a result of clients' greater alignment with wisdom – God's created design for how life is to be successfully lived – albeit for some only on a temporal level.

The issue of self-esteem was used in order to illustrate the 'logic' of diverse goals and practices within the field of Christian counselling, as these arise from different doctrinal assumptions, and so illustrate the importance of these assumptions in shaping goals and methods.

Lastly, Dueck's categories of 'analogy' and 'critique' were used as a means of illustrating how Christian counselling, if rooted in a wisdom Christology framework, would at some points be in agreement with modern secular therapeutic goals and methods, and at other times be distinct from them. This helps to avoid either wholesale absorption or an unduly defensive avoidance of modern scholarship, whether scientific or biblical.

Conclusion

In this last section a summary of the Waverley Model's strengths and weaknesses will be outlined and suggestions for further development offered. As stated at the outset of this book, Hughes himself understood that our knowledge of the soul is incomplete and in process ('on a journey') and as a result states, 'it is always good to question what we are saying and doing in relation to helping people with their problems' (see Hughes' opening quotation in the Introduction). This work has been carried out in a spirit of critical openness to the ongoing theological and practical development of Hughes' Waverley Model.

The Waverley Model presents a clear rationale of human motivation linked to the fulfilment of what Hughes called the spiritual longings for security, self-worth and significance. This type of approach focusing on relationality, especially with God, sits well amidst a long-established Augustinian theological and spiritual tradition. Hughes articulates his theory from the 'Fall' narrative of Genesis, which has the merit of taking the metanarrative of Scripture seriously, ie it starts where Scripture does – creation and Fall. It is also apparent that the Genesis account is not explicit about, or centred upon human needs. Hughes' theology may thus be regarded as creative and systematic, as he has explicitly sought to combine such theological data with modern psychological theory in an attempt to answer contemporary questions relating to the human condition. This latter point highlights one weakness regarding the starting point of Genesis. Unlike contemporary humanity, Adam and Eve did not start life as babies, and hence experience the developmental pathways through childhood that we all, of necessity, must do. Additionally, they did not develop amidst community as we do. Their 'dialogue' was exclusively (serpent apart) with God. For these reasons and more, some might prefer a theological method for deriving a model of personhood which starts with Christ.

With regard to Hughes' three core longings, differences in comparison to Crabb's model have been highlighted, where self-worth is derived from security and significance, rather than being a separate category. I have argued for the veracity of Crabb's position over Hughes', but would suggest that further work be carried out with regard to the precise relationship between these core longings. Are they discrete categories? Do they overlap? One possible corollary to Hughes' developmental outworking of our core longings (Chapter 2, 'Hughes and Social Context') is an ordering where security is primary and foundational, and self-worth a derivative of this security. As significance is articulated as developing last, this in turn may be conceived as being derived from self-worth. From this perspective, a different ordering altogether may arise, one in which chronological development is decisive, and thus each successive longing is founded upon and emerges out of its predecessor.

In general, terms/concepts such as 'thirsts' and 'longings' were defended by means of Christ's koilia teaching, as expressing an anthropological biblical theology and as a defence against critics who dislike a 'need theology'.

Hughes' model of health focuses upon God-dependence through a 'turn to Christ in faith' (repentance). I have suggested that this emphasis may be explained in part by Hughes' background as an evangelist and pastor. From the perspective of a Christian theistic world-view, this emphasis has been welcomed, yet at the same time acknowledgement has been given to its corollary which makes difficult the task of applying the model more generally beyond a pastoral context. However, this is the context for which it was first developed. A way through this apparent restriction of scope was offered, linked to a robust development of a wisdom Christology. This broadens our notion of repentance to include the benefits of realignment to the creation order – the Christ of wisdom (Chapter 2, 'Wisdom – A Broad Relationality').

The above broader notion of repentance, coupled with the emphasis of a functional rendering of imago Dei, provides a theological foundation from which a dialogue with science may be fostered when attempting to articulate models of health and pathology. This still leaves the question as to how theology and science might relate with regard to questions relevant to the above issues. In this book it has been argued that Scripture must retain a 'central' place. This stance was rooted in an understanding of salvation as outlined by McGrath, which leads us to expect that Scripture will offer profoundly relevant insights into personal problems of everyday living of the type that cause people to require counselling, for example guilt, anger, fear, identity issues, the need for love etc.

Beyond this general stance of theology's central role, more work needs to be carried out in relation to developing criteria which permit some flexibility in the relative authority of theological and scientific insights according to the specific psychological domain in view. In this work, I have offered a 'simple' test case where psychology must predominate, for instance ascertaining the extent and form of cognitive impairment following brain damage due to a car accident. I suspect there are numerous other specific issues that could be raised which also do not allow such a simple demarcation. A more nuanced criterion is thus required to help navigate our way through more 'subtle' issues relating to the overlap of spiritual and psychological, or issues which are deemed to be 'on the edges' of each domain.

It was noted that Hughes' emphasis upon repentance as a means of fostering healthy functioning can give rise to the view that personal sin alone is responsible for pathology. It has been shown (Chapter 1, 'Depravity') that such a reductionist view would not be an accurate portrayal of the Waverley Model. To this end, it has been highlighted that Hughes' inclusion of the physical area of functioning (which Crabb does not include), helps advance a broader conception of pathology beyond moral culpability. Hughes' conception, whilst including 'weakness' residing in our bodies as a causal agent of pathology, needs to be extended to incorporate systemic factors within the 'outside world' more clearly (both historical and contemporary). As a consequence, a more rounded biblical conception of sin which includes both individual (internal) and systemic (external) factors may be presented. This would better capture the impact that systemic powers (cultural and cosmic) have on our core spiritual self.

It was noted how Johnson's concept of 'moral fault' began to help express how 'weakness', whether bodily or systemic, might interface with personal agency and hence moral culpability. Further work is necessary in detailing how these two aspects operate together, beyond the general statement that both are involved. How can we determine in any given case which of these broad categories predominates? In which ways might each dynamically impact one another? A Pauline theology was also found to be helpful in articulating the connection between the outworking of personal sin and a systemic identification with Adam in his (the) Fall, and the subsequent malevolent powers reigning over us. These powers lead to pathological outcomes.

The concept of total depravity has been defended on the above grounds as expressing sin's pervasive presence – personal, historical and systemic. In this respect, the Waverley Model's emphasis on sin as a significant causal agent of pathology must not be lost; however, weakness occurring amidst systemic powers helps negate a view equating pathology with personal sin alone. Additionally, human essence has been defended as a 'relational substance', based upon the value of anthropocentric metaphors as essential descriptors of both God and humankind.

One practical outworking of a broad conception of both essence (substance/relationship) and pathology (individual/systemic) is that the traditional diagram of the Waverley Model needs amending to better portray 'the self' in continual dialogue with the 'outside world' – an open-ended self. This point arises throughout the pages of this book and provides a theological rationale for many research findings in the disciplines of Social Psychology, Neuroscience and Psychotherapy. Given this current book's restricted scope, a greater engagement with developments amongst the above three domains would further articulate a Christian approach to Psychotherapy, rooted in a dialogue between theology and contemporary scientific discovery. A further addition to the amended diagram of the Waverley Model is a portrayal of interior areas of functioning which are dynamically interrelated, if not coexistent. It has been noted that the traditional Waverley Model diagram gives the impression that each 'area of functioning' is discrete and might operate separately in relative isolation from the others, ie a modernist disection of the self (see Appendix A). However, the perforated concentric circles of the amended diagram better visually portray the interrelatedness of the various 'areas of functioning' (see Appendix B).

This work is not the only attempt at modifying the traditional Waverley Model's diagram; Kallmier's book on the Waverley Model offers his own diagram of dynamic interiority operating amidst the context of the outside world. It is quite possible that the postmodern zeitgeist of contemporary culture would permit a plurality of diagrams to operate together, each being part of an overall 'mosaic' of symbols attempting to capture that which one alone could not do. This book is an attempt to incorporate important issues that are at the heart of the Waverley Model in a manner which is relevant and usable for the twenty-first century.

Appendix A

The Traditional
Waverley Counselling Model

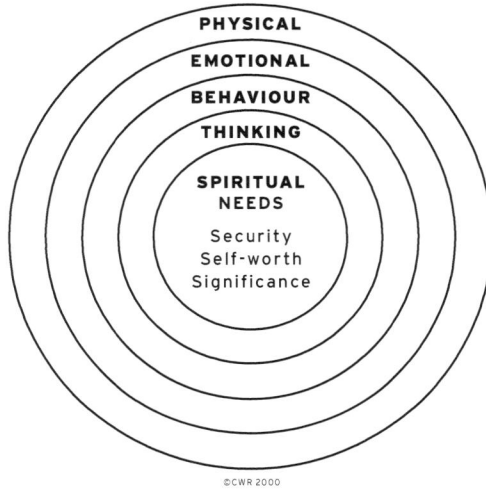

PHYSICAL

EMOTIONAL

BEHAVIOUR

THINKING

SPIRITUAL
NEEDS

Security
Self-worth
Significance

©CWR 2000

Appendix B

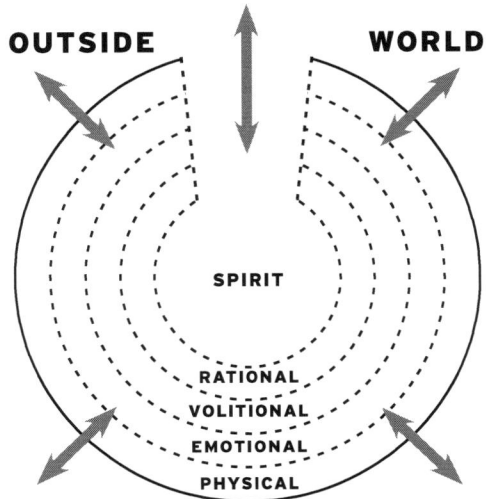

OUTSIDE

WORLD

SPIRIT

RATIONAL
VOLITIONAL
EMOTIONAL
PHYSICAL

Endnotes

For the extensive list of works utilised in the writing of this book, see the bibliography in Dr Owen Ashley's PhD, *A* Theological *and Practical Evaluation of* CWR'*s Waverley* Christian Counselling Model (Farnham: CWR, 2013).

Introduction

1. *Hughes*, S., unpublished letter responding to *The Summary of the Theology and Counselling Away–Day*, London School of Theology (LST) Friday 4 April 2003.

2. *Crabb*, L., *Understanding People: Deep Longings for Relationship* (Grand Rapids: Zondervan, 1987) p215.

3. *Yong*, A., *Spirit-Word-Community: Theological Hermeneutics in Trinitarian Perspective* (Oregon: Wipf & Stock, 2002) p183.

Chapter 1

4. *Hurding*, R.F., *The Bible and Counselling* (London: Hodder & Stoughton, 1992) p9.

5. Marshal, I.H., *Biblical Inspiration* (London: Hodder & Stoughton, 1982) p71.

6. Bloesch, D.G., 'The Primacy of *Scripture*', *The Authoritative Word: Essays on the Nature of Scripture* (ed.) McKim, D.K. (Grand Rapids: Eerdmans, 1983) p118.

7. Ward, K., *What the Bible Really Teaches: A Challenge for Fundamentalists* (London: SPCK, 2004) p15.

8. Hughes, *How to Help a Friend* (Eastbourne: Kingsway, 1981) p100.

9. Carson, D.A., *The Gagging of God: Christianity Confronts Pluralism* (Leicester: Apollos, 1996) p97.

10. Waverley Model Trainers' Notes (Farnham: *CWR*, 2000) p18.

11. Holmes, S.R., *Salvation* p713. *Dictionary of Biblical Theology*, (Grand Rapids: Baker, 1996) p701.

12. Waverley Model Trainers' Notes, p18.

13. Ibid.

14. Packer, J.I., '*Scripture*', *New Dictionary of Theology* (Leicester: IVP, 1988) p629.

15. Johnson, E.L. and Jones, S.L., (eds.), *Psychology and Christianity: Four Views* (Downers Grove: IVP, 2000) p38.

16. Myers, D. G., 'A Levels–of–Explanation View', *Johnson and Jones, Four Views*, p59.

17. Grenz, S.J, and Franke J.R., *Beyond Foundationalism* (Louisville: *John* Knox Press, 2001), p21.

18.   Moltmann, J., *Science and Wisdom* (London: SCM Press, 2003) p11.

19.   Collins, G.R., 'An *Integration* Response', *Johnson and Jones, Four Views*, p86.

20.   Faw, H.W., 'Wilderness and Promised *Integration*, The Quest for Clarity', *Journal of Psychology and Theology*, 26, 1998, pp147–158 cited by *Collins, Four Views*, p109.

21.   Roberts, R.C., *Psychology and Christianity: Four Views* (Illinois: IVP Academic, 2000), p138.

22.   Ibid., p150.

23.   Ibid., p152.

24.   Powli*son, Biblical*, p202. See Van Deurzen and Kenward, *Dictionary of Existential Psychotherapy and Counselling* (London: Sage, 2005) pp181–182.

25.   Vitz, P.C. and Felch, S.M., *The Self: Beyond the Postmodern Crisis*, (Delaware: ISI Books, 2006) p5.

26.   Collins, *The Biblical Basis of Christian Counselling for People Helpers* (Colorado Springs: Navigators Press, 2001) p97.

27.   Thiselton, A.C., *The Hermeneutics of Doctrine* (Grand Rapids: Eerdmans, 2007) p258.

28.   Richardson, A. and Bowden, J., (eds.), *A New Dictionary of Christian Theology* (London: SCM Press, 1983) p539.

29.   Hughes, *Christ Empowered Living* (Nashville: Broadman & Holman, 2001) p87.

30.   McFadyen, A., *Bound to Sin: Abuse, Holocaust and the Christian Doctrine of Sin* (Cambridge: CUP, 2000) p191.

31.   Ibid., p248.

32.   Ibid.

33.   Hill, C.C., 'Romans', Barton, J. and Muddiman, J., *The Oxford Bible Commentary*, (Oxford: OUniversityP, 2001) p1095.

34.   McFadyen, *Bound to Sin*, p126.

35.   Starkey, M., *What's Wrong: Understanding Sin Today* (Oxford: The *Bible* Reading Fellowship, 2001) p104.

36.   *Waverley Model* Trainers' Notes, p50.

37.   Ibid.

38.   Hughes, *Christ Empowered Living*, p93.

39.   Johnson, *Sin*, p223.

40.   Starkey, *What's Wrong*, pp77–78.

41.   Biddle, M.E., *Missing the Mark: Sin and its Consequences in Biblical Theology* (Nashville: Abingdon Press, 2005) pxviii.

42.   Schreiner, T., *Paul Apostle of God's Glory in Christ: A Pauline Theology* (Leicester: IVP, 2001) p149.

43.   Waverley Model Trainers' Notes, p28.

44.   Grenz, S.J., *The Social God and the Relational Self: A Trinitarian Theology of the Imago Dei* (Louisville, Westminste: *John* Knox Press, 2001) p142.

45.   Ferguson, S.B. *New Dictionary of Theology*, p328.

46.   Calvin, J., *The Institutes of Christian Religion* 1, 15.3, McNeil, J.T., (ed.), Battles, F.L., (tr.) (Philadelphia: Westminster Press, 1960) p162.

47.   Hartley, J.E., *Genesis: New International Biblical Commentary* (Pea*body*: Hendrick*son*, 2000) p53.

48.   Berkhof, L., *Systematic Theology* (Edinburgh: Banner of *Truth*, 1939) p56.

49.   Hebblethwaite, B., *'Anthropomorphism'*, Richard*son*, A. and Bowden, J. (eds.), *A New Dictionary of Christian Theology*, (London: SCM Press, 1983) p26.

50.   Berkhof, Systematic Theology, p65.

51.   Berkouwer, G.C., *Man: The image of God Studies in Dogmatics* (Grand Rapids: Eerdmans, 1984) p70.

52.   Smail, T., *Like Father Like Son: The Trinity Imaged in our Humanity* (Milton Keynes: Peternoster Press, 2005) p162.

53.   Barth, K., *Church Dogmatics* Volume III, (Edinburgh: T. and T. Clark, 1961) p246.

54.   Grenz, *The Social God and the Relational Self*, p162.

55.   Brunner, E., *Man in Revolt: A Christian Anthropology* (London: Lutterworth, 1939) p95.

56.   Shults, L.F., *Reforming Theological Anthropology: After the Philosophical Turn to Relationality* (Grand Rapids: Eerdmans, 2003) p234.

57.   Middleton, J.R., *The Liberating Image: The Imago Dei in Genesis 1* (Grand Rapids: Brazos Press, 2005) p266.

58.   McFadyen, A., *The Call to Personhood* (Cambridge: CUP, 1990) p24.

59.   Ibid., pp22,27,29.

60.   Ibid., p77.

61.   Witherington III, B., *1 and 2 Thessalonians: A Socio-Rhetorical Commentary* (Grand Rapids: Eerdmans, 2006) p103.

62.   Goldingay, J., *'Biblical Narrative and Systematic Theology,'* Green, J.B. and Turner, M., (eds.), *Between Two Horizons: Spanning New Testament Studies and Systematic Theology*, (Grand Rapids: Eerdmans, 2000) p141.

63. Vitz, P.C., *Limning the Psyche* (Grand Rapids: Eerdmans, 1997), p31. *John* Paul II and the Pope Benedict XVI are also quoted as holding this position.

64. Ibid., p32.

65. Smail, T., *Like Father Like Son*, p109.

66. Wright, N.T., *The Resurrection of the Son of God*, (London: SPCK, 2003) p283.

67. Waverley Model Trainers' Notes, p27.

68. Hughes, S., *The Seven Laws of Spiritual Success* (Farnham: *CWR*, 2002) p115 citing Broughton, K.D., *The Everlasting God* (Darlington: *Evangelical* Press, 1982).

69. Pannenberg, W., *Human Nature, Election and History* (Philadelphia: Westminster Press, 1977) p28.

Chapter 2

70. Waverley Model Trainers' Notes, p30

71. Caird, G.B., *The Language and Imagery of the Bible* (London: Duckworth, 1980) p178.

72. Heschel, A.J., *The Prophets* Vol. 2 (Grand Rapids: Harper and Row, 1982) p51.

73. Crabb,L.J., *Understanding People*, p112. It is not without relevance that *Crabb*'s book *Understanding People* is subtitled 'Deep *Longings* for Relationship'.

74. Ryken, L.; Wilhoit, J.C. and Longman III, T., (eds.), *Dictionary of Biblical Imagery* (Downers Grove: IVP, 1998) p763.

75. Crabb, L.J., *Connecting: Healing for Ourselves and Our Relationships* (Nahville: W. Publishing Group, 1997) ppxvi – xvii.

76. Moltmann, J., *Science and Wisdom*, p149.

77. Hughes, S., *Christ Empowered Living*, p135.

78. Waverley Model Trainers' Notes, p30.

79. Hughes, S, *Christ Empowered Living*, p34.

80. Hughes, S., *How to Help a Friend*, p42.

81. Waverley Model Trainers' Notes, p32.

82. Hughes, S., *Christ Empowered Living*, p100.

83. Waverley Model Trainers' Notes, p30.

84. Hughes, S., *Christ Empowered Living*, p100.

85. Brunner, E., 'The *Christian* Understanding of Man', *The Christian Understanding of Man*, Jessop, T.E., (London: Allen Ltds, 1938) p146.

86. Hughes, S., *How to Help a Friend*, p38.

87. Hughes, S., *Christ Empowered Living*, p102.

88. Ibid.

89. Bandura, A., *Aggression: A Social Learning Analysis* (New Jersey: Prentice Hall, 1973) p113.

90. Bandura, A., *Social Foundations of Thought and Action: A Social Cognitive Theory* (New Jersey, Prentice Hall, 1986) p21.

91. Martin, R.A. and Hill, P.C., 'Social Learning Theory,' *Benner*, D.G. and *Hill*, P.C., *Baker Encyclopaedia of Psychology and Counselling* (2nd ed.), (Grand Rapids: Baker Books, 1999) p1139

92. Hearnshaw, L.S., *The Shaping of Modern Psychology: An Historical Introduction* (London: Routledge and Kegan, Paul, 1987), p241

93. Gunton, C.E., *The One, The Three and The Many: God, Creation and the Culture of Modernity: The 1992 Bampton Lectures* (New York: CUP, 1993) p147.

94. Crabb, L.J., *Understanding People*, p215.

95. Erikson, E., *Childhood and Society* (2nd ed.) (New York: W.W. Norton, 1963) p255.

96. Hughes, S., *Christ Empowered Living*, p104.

97. Crabb, L.J., *Understanding People*, p93.

98. Ibid.

99. Ibid., p94.

100. Adams, J.E., *A Theology of Christian Counselling* (Grand Rapids: Zondervan, 1974) p115.

101. Lincoln, A.T., *The Gospel According to Saint John* (New York: Hendrickson Publishers, Inc., 2005), p257.

102. Schnackenburg, R., *The Gospel, According to St John*, (London: Burns and Oats, 1980) p156. Keene, R.C.S., *The Gospel of John: A Commentary* Vol. 1 (Massachusetts: Hendrickson Publishers, 2003) pp721–726.

103. Brown, P., *Augustine of Hippo: A Biography* (London: Faber and Faber, 1967) p210.

104. Bailie, G., 'The Imitative *Self*: The Contribution of Rene Girard', Vitz, P.C. and Felch, S.M., (eds.), *The Self* (Delaware: ISI Books, 2006) p14.

105. Ibid., p14.

106. Augustine, *Confessions of St. Augustine* , Gill, T. (ed.), Outler, A.C., (tr.) 1950s, (New York: Sheed and Ward, 1942/1985) p190.

107. Roberts, R.C., 'Parameters of a *Christian Psychology*', Roberts, R.C. and Talbot, M.R. (eds.) *Limning the Psyche: Explorations in Christian Psychology* (Oregon: Wipf and Stock, 2003) p84.

108. Brown, P., *Augustine of Hippo*, p211 citing St *Augustine*.

109. Vanhoozer, K.J, '*Human Being Individual* and *Social*', *Gunton*, C., (ed.), *The Cambridge Companion to Christian Doctrine* (Cambridge: CUP, 1997) p158.

110. Ibid., p159.

111. Grenz, S.J., *The Social God and the Relational Self*, p61.

112. McFadyen, A., *Bound to Sin*, p203.

113. Waverley Model Trainers' Notes, p32.

114. Niebuhr, H.R., *Christ and Culture* (New York: Harper *Collins*, 1951/2001) p256.

115. Roth, K.L., 'The *Psychology* and Counselling of Richard *Baxter* (1615–1691)', *Journal of Psychology and Christianity*, Vol. 17, 4, 1998, p322.

116. Baxter, R., *The Reformed Pastor* (Edinburgh: Banner of *Truth Trust*, 1656/1974) pp120, 121.

117. Scougal, H., *The Life of God in the Soul of Man* (Fearn: Christian Focus, 1996) p73.

118. Ibid.

119. Gunton, C.E., '*Trinity, Ontology* and *Anthropology*: Towards a Renewal of the *Doctrine* of the *Imago Dei*', Schwobel, C. and *Gunton*, C.E. (eds.), *Persons Divine and Human* (Edinburgh: T. and T. Clark, 1991) p48.

120. McFarlane, G., 'Living on the Edge – Moving Towards the Centre: the Place of *Jesus Christ* in our Quest for *Personhood*', *Evangelical Quarterly*, *Marshall*, I.H. and Lane, A.N.S. (eds.), Vol. 78, 1, 2006, p44.

121. Ibid., p48.

122. Smail, T., *Like Father Like Son*, p128.

123. Tennant, F.R., *The Origin and Propagation of Sin* (Cambridge: CUP, 2012), p82.

124. McFadyen, *The Call to Personhood*, p318. *McFadyen* gives specific theories outlining the connection between the *development* of a particular '*self*' and our *relational* environment.

125. Clifford, R.J., *Proverbs* (Louisville: Westminster *John* Knox Press, 1999) pp196–197.

126. Waltke, B.K., *The Book of Proverbs* (Grand Rpaids: Eerdmans, 2005) p203. See also Murphy, R.E., *Proverbs: Word Biblical Commentary*, (Nashville: Thomas Nel*son*, 1988) p165: Early training produces fruit in later life.

127. Harris, A., 'Psychic Envelopes and *Sonorous* Baths: citing the *Body* in Relational Theory and Clinical Practice', Aron, L. and Sommer-*Anderson*, F., (eds.), *Relational Perspectives on the Body* (New Jersey: The Analytic Press, 1998) p61.

Chapter 3

128. Hughes, S., *Christ Empowered Living*, pxv.

129. Adams, J.E., *How to Help People Change: The Four Step Biblical Process* (Grand Rapids: Zondervan, 1986) p142.

130. Dunn, J.D.G., *World Biblical Commentary: Romans 1–8* (Dallas: Thomas Nelson, 1988) p39.

131. Barth, K., *The Epistle to the Romans* (London: OUP, 1933) p424.

132. Hughes, S., *Christ Empowered Living*, pxv.

133. McFadyen, A., *The Call to Personhood*, p58.

134. Kruse, C., *John*, (Nottingham: Inter-Varsity Press, 2008), p294.

135. Niebuhr, H.R., *Christ and Culture*, pxiii. See also Hunter, A., *Wisdom Literature*, (London: SCM Press, 2006) p23.

136. Ford, D.F., *Christian Wisdom: Desiring God and Learning in Love*, (Cambridge: CUP, 2007) p57.

137. Schnabel, E.J., '*Wisdom*', Alexander, T.D. and Rosner, B.S., (eds.), *New Dictionary of Biblical Theology*, (Nottingham: Inter-Varsity Press, 2000) p847.

138. Ford, D.F., *Christian Wisdom*, p27.

139. Bobgan, M. and *Bobgan*, D., *Psychoheresy: The Psychological Seduction of Christianity* (Santa Barbara: Eastgate, 1987). p103.

140. Volf, M., *Exclusion and Embrace: A Theological Exploration of Identity, Otherness and Reconciliation* (Nashville: Abingdon Press, 1996) p115.

141. Fee, G.D. and Stuart, D., *How to Read the Bible for all it's Worth: A Guide to Understanding the Bible*, (2nd ed.), (Grand Rapids, Zondervan, 1993) p206.

142. Osborne, G.R., *The Hermeneutical Spiral: A Comprehensive Introduction to Biblical Interpretation* (Downers Grove: IVP, 1991) p191.

143. Deane-Drummond, C., *Wonder and Wisdom: Conversations in Science, Spirituality and Theology* (London: Darton, Longman and Todd, 2006) p88.

144. Webb, W.J., *Slaves, Women and Homosexuals: Exploring the Hermeneutics of Cultural Analysis* (Downers Grove: IVP, 2001) p57.

145. Ibid., p58.

146. Deane-Drummond, C., *Wonder and Wisdom* pp 93–94.

147. Adams, J.E., *A Theology of Christian Counselling*, pxii: 'We have often heard it said that: "All *truth* is *God*'s *truth*."'

148. Dunn, J.D.G., *Christology in the Making: A New Testament Inquiry into the Origins of the Doctrine*

of the Incarnation (London: SCM Press, 1989) p105.

149. Hughes, S., *The Seven Laws of Spiritual Success*, p11.

150. Ibid., p12.

Chapter 4

151. Hughes, S., *Christ Empowered Living*, p xv.

152. Waverley Model Trainers' Notes, p28

153. Ibid., p33.

154. Craigie, P.C.; Kelley, P.H. and Drinkard, J.F., *Word Biblical Commentary: Jeremiah 1–25* (Dallas: Word Books, 1991) p28.

155. Osborne, G.R., *The Hermeneutical Spiral*, p208.

156. Waverley Model Trainers' Notes, p33.

157. Pannenberg, W., *Anthropology in Theological Perspective* (Edinburgh: T. and T. Clark, 1985) p225.

158. Freud, S., *An Outline of Psychoanalysis* (London: Hogarth, 1940) p5.

159. Greenberg, J.R. and Mitchell, S.A., *Object Relations in Psychoanalytic Theory* (Massachusetts: Howard University Press, 2000) p44.

160. Gomez, L., *An Introduction to Object Relations* (London: Free Association Books, 1997) p4.

161. Fairbairn, W.R.D., 'The Repression and Return of Bad Objects, with Special Reference to the War Neuroses', Buckley, P. (ed.) *Essential Papers on Object Relations*, (New York: New York University Press, 1986) p103.

162. Looker, T., 'Mama, Why Don't Your *Feet* Touch the Ground?: Staying with the *Body* and the *Healing* Moment in *Psychoanalysis*', Aron, L. and Sommer *Anderson*, F., (eds.), *Relational Perspectives on the Body* (London: The Analytic Press, 1998) p247.

163. Fairbairn, W.R.D., 'The Repression and Return of Bad Objects, with Special Reference to the War Neuroses', pp102–103.

164. Bowlby, J., *Attachment and Loss: Separation, Anger and Anxiety* Vol. 2, (London: Hogarth Press, 1973) p236.

165. Bowlby, J., *The Making and Breaking of Affectional Bonds* (London: Routledge, 1989) pp161–162.

166. Gerhardt, S., *Why Love Matters* (New York: Routledge, 2014), p38 citing Chugani et al, 2001.

167. Green, J.B., *Body, Soul and Human Life: The Nature of Humanity in the Bible* (Grand Rapids: Baker Academic, 2008) p63.

168. Johnson, E.L., '*Human Agency* and its *Social* Formation', Roberts, R.C., and Talbot, M. R., (eds.), *Limning the Psyche: Explorations in Christian Psychology* (Oregon: Wipf and Stock, 2003) p152.

169. Jones, S.L. and Butman, R.E., *Modern Psychotherapies: A Comprehensive Guide* (Downers Grove: IVP, 1991) p107.

170. Palmer, S.L., '*Christian* Life and Theories of *Human* Nature', *Green*, J.B. and Palmer, S.L., *In Search of the Soul: Four Views of the Mind-Body Problem* (Downers Grove: IVPress, 2005) p214.

Chapter 5

171. Joyce, P. and Sills, C., *Skills in Gestalt Counselling and Psychotherapy* (London: Sage, 2001) p57.

172. Ibid., p59.

173. Waverley Model Trainers' Notes, p52.

174. Ibid. p69.

175. Ibid.

176. Ibid.

177. Hughes, S., *The Pocket Guide for People Helpers* (Farnham: *CWR*, 2004) p8.

178. Kallmier, R., *Caring and Counselling: An Introduction to the Waverley Model of Counselling* (Farnham: *CWR*, 2011) p191.

179. Jones, S.L. and Butman, R.E., *Modern Psychotherapies*, p59.

180. Williams, R., *On Christian Theology: Challenges in Contemporary Theology* (Oxford: Blackwell, 2000) p110.

181. Yong, A., *Beyond the Impasse: Toward a Pneumatological Theology of Religions* (Grand Rapids: Baker Academic, 2003) p131.

182. Olthuis, J.H., *The Beautiful Risk: A New Psychology of Loving and Being Loved* (Wipf and Stock, 2006) p102.

183. Williams, R., *On Christian Theology*, pp125–126.

184. Crabb, L.J., *Understanding People*, p29.

185. Hilber, J.W., '*Old Testament Wisdom* and the *Integration* Debate in *Christian* Counselling', *Bibliotheca Sacra 155*, October–December 1988, p417.

186. Yong, A., *Beyond the Impasse*, p130.

187. Boa, K., *Conformed to His Image: Biblical and Practical Approaches to Spiritual Formation* (Grand Rapids: Zondervan, 2001) p317.

188.   Schuller, R.H., *Self-esteem: The New Reformation* (Waco: Word Books, 1982) p69.

189.   Adams, J.E., *The Biblical View of Self-Esteem, Self-Love, Self-Image* (Eugene: Harvest House, 1986) p118.

190.   McGrath, J. and *McGrath*, A., *Self-Esteem: The Cross and Christian Confidence* (Nottingham: IVP, 2001) p11.

191.   Stott, J., *The Cross of Christ* (Nottingham: IVP, 1986), p319.

192.   Cooper, T.D., *Sin, Pride and Self-Acceptance: The Problem of Identity in Theology and Psychology* (Downers Grove: IVP, 2003) p47.

193.   Fouque, P. and Glachan, M., 'The Impact of *Christian* Counselling on Survivors of Sexual Abuse', *Counselling Psychology Quarterly*, Vol. 13, 2, 2000, pp201–220.

194.   Hilber, J.W. *'Old Testament Wisdom* and the *Integration* Debate in *Christian* Counselling', p 418.

195.   Hurding, R.F., *The Bible and Counselling*, p47.

196.   Dueck, A., *Athens* (London: Harper *Collins*, 1994) p8.

197.   Egan G., *The Skilled Helper: A Problem-Management and Opportunity-Development Approach to Helping* (Australia (n.p): Thom*son* Brooks/Cole, 2007) p307.

198.   Olthuis, J.H., *The Beautiful Risk*, p44.

199.   Watkins, C., *'Transference* Phenomena in the Counselling Situation', Dryden, Windy, (ed.), *Key Issues for Counselling in Action* (London: Sage, 1988) p73.

200.   Rogers, C.R., *On Becoming a Person: A Therapist's View of Psychotherapy* (London: Constable, 1961) p27.

201.   Forshaw, O., *Personhood and Christianity in Psychodynamic and Corporate Perspective* (Cambridge: Lutterworth Press, 2010) p78.

202.   Ford, D.F., *Christian Wisdom*, p137.

203.   Beck, A.T., *Cognitive Therapy of Depression* (New York: The Guilford Press, 1979), p45.

204.   Rogers, C.R. *On Becoming a Person*, pp16–20. *Jacobs*, M., *Psychodynamic Counselling in Action* (London: Sage, 2004) pp16–18.

205.   Dueck, A., *Athens*, p7.

206.   *Ethical Framework for Good Practice in Counselling and Psychotherapy* (Rugby: *BACP*, 2002) p3.

Subject Index

Index of Authors, Names and Biblical Books